On the cover:
Front: France chair, 1956, courtesy of House of Finn Juhl.
Back: Interior by Amy Lau, photo by Kim Sargent; Arne Vodder model 211
sideboard, photo by Jennifer Roch for Adore Modern.

First published in the United Kingdom in 2017 by
Thames & Hudson Ltd, 181A High Holborn, London WC1V 7QX

Reprinted in 2019

This book was designed and produced by
The Bright Press, an imprint of the Quarto Group
The Old Brewery, 6 Blundell Street,
London N7 9BH, United Kingdom.

British Library Cataloguing-in-Publication Data
A catalogue record for this book is available from the British Library

ISBN 978-0-500-51957-8

Printed and bound in China

To find out about all our publications, please visit **www.thamesandhudson.com**.
There you can subscribe to our e-newsletter, browse or download our current
catalogue, and buy any titles that are in print.

A ROOM BY ROOM GUIDE

MID-CENTURY MODERN at HOME

DC Hillier

Contents

Preface

In the mid 1990s, I was at art school studying film and media. Living the life of a student, I was often strapped for cash. Still requiring the basics of life, which included some furniture, I hit the flea markets and second-hand shops to find a few inexpensive items for my apartment. This was when I first began noticing pieces that were different, that stood out from the rest of the faux Victorian and revivalist-styled items of furniture. There were simple yet compelling chairs with clean lines and a purposeful stance. There were also unadorned sofas, low to the floor, offering comfort without clutter, and light fixtures that looked as if they were from the set of some fantastic science-fiction film. I became enamoured with this modernist style, and particularly with post-Second World War modernism, which today is commonly referred to as mid-century modern. At college I began taking a few design courses, and while I loved studying film, modern design quickly became my new passion. I devoured every book and magazine I could find on the subject and soon was studying design full time.

After graduating I worked in several fields of design, including graphic and packaging design.

While these fields offered satisfying work, my real desire was to make the leap into interior design, where I could couple my design work with my knowledge and love for mid-century modern.

In 2004 I got my first interior-design commission and I was able to convince the client to include as many quality mid-century modern pieces as possible. At the time, mid-century modern was not the buzz phrase it would go on to become, and often clients simply did not know what it was. More often than not, they referred to it as 'old fashioned'. Today, mid-century modern abounds, with larger retailers all seeming to offer furniture and accessories in this style.

On the one hand, I think it is wonderful that a style I am passionate about has become popular and easier to acquire. However, there can be something off about many of these mass-market pieces; they may be poorly made or simply copies of well-known classic designs. My hope is that, with this book, you'll be able to discern between the real and the fake, and discover how authentic mid-century modern can be just as affordable as the copies, and achievable for your own home.

▸ *A period property styled with an array of mid-century modern furniture and accessories. Wherever you live, by using this book you can create your own mid-century modern home.*

1. INTRODUCING MID-CENTURY MODERN

What is mid-century modern?

During the mid 20th century there were various schools of thought in art and design. The designers and architects of the Bauhaus, for example, adhered to a philosophy of 'form follows function', which led the way for movements such as European minimalism and the International Style. In the Scandinavian countries, the craftsmanship approach to furniture design led the way for the fluid designs of organic rationalism. And in North America a new industrialized modernism was emerging following the post-war boom. However, there never did exist a movement called 'mid-century modern'. This term, first popularized by author Cara Greenberg in her 1983 book of the same name, is simply an umbrella term that covers a wide gamut of the various movements and 'isms' in 20th-century modernism.

Difficult to define

Trying to define what is or isn't a mid-century modern design may prove to be somewhat reductive. It is far too easy to become bogged down and pedantic when it comes to labelling mid-century modern in black-and-white terms. Certainly, we know when it is, and many people believe it encompasses all modern design between 1945 to around 1970. However, when you consider all the various approaches and schools of thought during these thirty or so years of design it becomes immediately apparent that there is no one look that is definitively mid-century modern.

It is easy to spot post-war Danish modern, minimalism, or American modern and, despite their differences, each one of these styles falls under the term 'mid-century modern'. Such variety of international influences makes defining 'mid-century modern' difficult. There were no set parameters followed by any of these design movements, and in terms of period many overlap, as designers borrowed from and responded to what had gone on before them.

Simplicity in design

To educate oneself on the evolution of the key movements of 20th-century modernist design is to understand and recognize mid-century modern in all its forms. It therefore helps to first understand the meaning of 'modernism', a term applied to everything from art to buildings. At the core of modernist principles is simplicity. Whether found in the minimalist styling of a Dieter Waeckerlin cabinet or in the restrained fluidity of a Finn Juhl chair, there is never anything 'unnecessary' about a modern design; there is always just enough. The approach to simplicity in design is certainly nothing new, not even to the modernist, but the desire to create a simple piece of elegant furniture was not just an academic exercise. Rather, designers sought to create timeless designs that would serve for decades, looking beyond ideological trends and whatever was 'in' at the time. This is why the mid-century modern style endures.

◄ *A typical mid-century modern room may include pieces by various different designers. Collections, and therefore interiors, can be as eclectic as one wishes.*

◄◄ *The Diamond chair, designed by Harry Bertoia for Knoll, is a classic example of mid-century modern design.*

The evolution of modernism in the 20th century

The often tumultuous 20th century was a period of creative, artistic, social and cultural change and upheaval. The public forums of art, design, and architecture were deeply affected by the impact of two devastating wars, followed by the growing worldwide unease and uncertainty caused by the Cold War, as well as by changing social norms and the development of civil rights. Whether for social or cultural, economic or political reasons, design in the 20th century evolved at a blistering pace. Here are a few key movements that laid the ground for the development of mid-century modern design.

The Arts and Crafts movement

Modernism as a movement in design, art and architecture has its roots in the latter part of the 19th century with the tenets of the Arts and Crafts movement. It lasted from about 1850 to 1910, beginning in Britain and later spreading to Europe and the United States. The Arts and Crafts movement valued quality and simplicity of form, and rebuked the products and processes of the 'machine-made' decorative arts of the late 19th century, which they believed were 'impoverished' in quality. As well as an aesthetic challenge, the movement made a social call to action against the working conditions in which these pieces were made.

At the Great Exhibition of 1851 in London, countless factory-made items – shown with pride by the manufacturers and received with great delight by the spectators – were scorned by the craftsmen of the period. Their perception of the furniture on display was that it was unnecessarily ornamented (a feature that would come to define Victorian style), ignored the quality and nature of the materials used, and of poor quality. This idea that the ornamental quality of a piece should be secondary to build quality and function demonstrates how the Arts and Crafts movement was among the pioneers of the modern idea, decades ahead of its time.

◄ *A fireplace in Whitewick Manor, near Wolverhampton, UK. The style is typical of the Arts and Crafts movement.*

◄ *A desk inspired by the geometric Art Nouveau style of Charles Rennie Mackintosh.*

The far-reaching influence of the Arts and Crafts movement is a testament to its enduring ideals. Whether it was the Scottish school, led by Charles Rennie Mackintosh, La Libre Esthétique (Free Aesthetic) of the French, or the Craftsman Style of North America, the idea of well-made, simple furniture that would serve its purpose for decades would become one of the core beliefs of the post-war modern movements.

Art Nouveau

Art Nouveau was an international style popular between 1890 and 1910. As is often the case, the Art Nouveau movement was a reactionary one. Decades after the rise of the Arts and Crafts movement the practitioners of Art Nouveau yearned for something new (although the two styles did briefly coexist). Taking influence from plants and flowers, and even from the softly drifting lines of cigarette smoke, the creations of this period are distinctly fluid, elegant and light.

Considered to be a 'total' art movement, Art Nouveau not only influenced architecture and the decorative arts but also painting and sculpture.

Taking its name from the art gallery Maison de l'Art Nouveau, operated by Franco-German art dealer Siegfried Bing, Art Nouveau was the first truly international style. Improvements in printing technologies made publishing the ideas of a design movement much more affordable, and allowed the various manifestations of the Art Nouveau school to reach a wide audience. The designers, architects, and artists from this group brought to the fore the modern impulse and necessity to explore and experiment, never limiting one's imagination, and thereby contributed to the evolution of modernism.

▲ *An interior from the Haus am Horn, a building erected and furnished as a part of the Weimar Bauhaus exhibition in 1923.*

The Deutscher Werkbund

The Deutscher Werkbund (German Crafts Association) was a collective of artists, designers, architects and business firms established in 1907 by Viennese architect Joseph Maria Olbrich. Members of the Werkbund included Ludwig Mies van der Rohe and Eliel Saarinen. The Werkbund influenced modern architecture and industrial design, perhaps most notably with the later establishment of the Bauhaus school of design.

Initially started as a way of connecting designers with manufacturers to make German-made products more competitive worldwide, the Werkbund was mostly focused on efficient, simple and well-made German products and design. With the manufacturers wanting low production costs, and the designers wanting good-quality design, the Werkbund introduced to the world the concept of 'design solution' over decorative art.

While most movements in modern design were a reaction to the movements that preceded them, the Werkbund was eager to take the best of all existing styles and techniques and apply these lessons to their mandate, which borrowed heavily from the Arts and Crafts movement. However, it was formed at a time when Europe was going through tremendous social upheaval. The Werkbund's first major work, a theatre for the

1914 Cologne Exhibition designed by Belgian architect Henry van de Velde, was closed and torn down due to the outbreak of the First World War. While there were more noteworthy projects produced in the decades that followed, the Deutscher Werkbund was eventually shut down by the Nazis in 1938.

The legacy of the Deutscher Werkbund cannot be overstated. The concept of well-made, easy-to-produce and affordable products is at the core of modernism. In fact, the Deutscher Werkbund was the seed that bore the 'less is more' credo that would go on to define the Bauhaus school and the International Style, and would influence modern design for decades to come.

Art Deco

Contemporary with, but often stylistically in contrast to the minimalist approach of Bauhaus was Art Deco. Bold, bright and brief, the Art Deco style reached into every facet of early 20th-century living, including architecture, automobile design, jewellery, fashion and graphic design. Bringing together a miscellany of several international styles, some seemingly at odds, the desire was to be modern. Inspired by the brash geometric

◀ *A table lamp, typical of Art Nouveau style.*

▶ *An Art Deco sideboard.*

patterns found in Cubism, and the aesthetics of Japan, India and Persia, the Art Deco movement was focused on the exotic and the luxurious. Detractors of the Art Deco style, with its bold colours and forms, derided it as being over-the-top and lacking substance, while proponents embraced its humanity.

With the First World War a recent memory, the sensual figurative art and sculpture, sleek products and exciting architecture of Art Deco offered an escape from a sometimes brutal world. It was the Roaring Twenties, the age of flappers and American jazz music, and Art Deco served as a perfect backdrop. The legacy of Art Deco is in its playful approach to design, the willingness to try new materials, embracing excitement for its own sake. Such ebullience, however, would come to a quick end with the start of the Second World War in 1939.

Post-war modernism in the United States

The Second World War had a devastating impact on much of the world. With most of Europe in ruins and with the onset of the Cold War, thoughts of modern design seemed rather trivial to the average person trying to put their life back together. However, in the United States it was also an economic boom time, and the American public was eager to put the past behind them and enjoy a new prosperity. With cheap and plentiful resources, and a manufacturing sector that had revved into high gear to keep up with wartime demand, this new global power was ripe for its own design and industrial revolution.

Automobile manufacturers, no longer producing for the war effort, were once again designing and making cars for the public. These cars were in the same style as the pre-war models until Harley Earl, designer at General Motors, created the 1948 Cadillac; the first American car

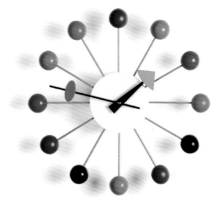

◄ *Kaufmann Desert House in Palm Springs, which was designed by American architect Richard Neutra in 1946, soon after the Second World War.*

▼ *The famous Ball wall clock from George Nelson & Associates, manufactured by the Howard Miller Clock Company.*

to have tail fins. The 1948 Cadillac would go on to capture the public imagination and Earl, who went on to design further outrageous concept cars for automotive shows, would further fuel the public's desire for the new.

Modern was quickly becoming the go-to style of the American public. Soon, with the rapid expansion into the suburbs, architects, designers and manufacturers were busy keeping up with the demand for modern design. Several prominent designers took an approach of good design aimed at the masses. Charles and Ray Eames, for instance, experimented with inexpensive materials and wood lamination processes with the goal of creating affordable and well-made furniture. Eero Saarinen introduced the ideas of organic rationalism, freeing modernist design from its tendency towards rigidity. George Nelson & Associates, a firm of several designers, were creating countless modern classics, from

furniture to clocks, most of them being produced by Howard Miller in Zeeland, Michigan. George Nakashima introduced a new American craft movement that combined traditional Japanese woodworking techniques with a modern American aesthetic. Architects such as Archibald Quincy Jones, Richard Neutra and John Lautner were redefining the American domestic experience. The breadth and range of modernism in America during the post-war period was huge.

Design solutions for Europe

In Europe during the post-war period, there was little of the exuberance seen in America. Europe was focused on rebuilding the continent and moving on from a long and devastating conflict. However, there were some designers who, borrowing from Bauhaus, saw a chance to demonstrate that good design can be made cheaply and built quickly. They saw design as offering solutions to civic need and believed that the time for the democratization of modern design had arrived. Le Corbusier, who was already sixty years old by the end of the Second World War, and well established as an architect and designer, was eager to demonstrate the idea that design can be a conduit for easing some societal ills. In 1947, he designed his Unité d'Habitation (also called Cité Radieuse) in Marseille, which would go on to become the model of high-density urban housing for decades to come.

Meanwhile, a unique style was developing in Italy, which had been cut off from the rest of the world by the edict of Benito Mussolini, that all Italian products should be designed and made by Italians for Italians. Modern designers in Italy during this period saw design as a statement of rebellion against the anti-intellectual Fascist regime. Influential architect and designer Gio Ponti would find his greatest success once Italy was reopened to the rest of the world following the end of the Second World War.

In the Scandinavian countries, designers such as Hans J. Wegner, Aksel Bender Madsen, Finn Juhl, Børge Mogensen and Nanna Ditzel were

▲ *The Unité d'Habitation in Berlin, also known as the Corbusierhaus, designed by Le Corbusier.*

continuing in the craftsman tradition of quality furniture that respected natural materials. Sculpted curvilinear frames and leather upholstery would define the timeless look of modern Scandinavian design. But there were some designers who wanted to create a new style vocabulary, and with the designs by Poul Volther and Poul Kjærholm, new materials such as steel and alternative forms entered the canon of Scandinavian modern design.

As time progressed, several styles emerged that would become enfolded in the broader catch-all term of 'mid-century modern' design. With the development of plastics, a pop-modern style, briefly popular in Italy and France in the late 1960s, played with the ideas of Futurism and, in some cases, social dystopia. Often these designs were experiments in material processes and exercises in academic theory. Meanwhile, concrete was becoming the signature material of the Brutalist architecture movement and a new 'socialist modern' was emerging from the 1960s. In Italy playfulness gave way to a 'sexualizing' of design with notions of communal living and a free-love social order. Modernism was an expanding and inclusive field, and there were many ideas, approaches and practices in post-war Europe – some more successful than others.

▼ *A wall-mounted panel and shelving system, 46 sofa, Nyhavn table and various light fixtures, all by Scandinavian designer Finn Juhl.*

The key movements of mid-century modern design

Like the Art Nouveau movement of the late 19th and early 20th centuries, mid-century modern can to an extent be considered a 'total' style in the sense that it encompasses architectural, interior, product and graphic design. However, there are subtle, often culturally influenced differences between the various approaches to mid-century modern adopted by designers around the world. For example, European designers were influenced directly by the utilitarian approach of Bauhaus, while post-war prosperity in the United States meant American modernists were arguably more adventurous in their use of new materials and indulgent styling.

International Style

International Style emerged in Europe following the Second World War. Taking influence from the Bauhaus movement, function was paramount, as well as clean and almost utilitarian materials. The later driving forces behind the International Style movement included architects and designers such as Le Corbusier, Charlotte Perriand, Jean Prouvé and, most notably, Ludwig Mies van der Rohe.

America

In the United States during the prosperous post-war period, the prevailing thought was 'anything new is good', and American architects and designers soon found themselves with a buying public eager for the 'new look'. American modernism, while still emphasizing function and simplicity, was a bit more liberated than the European style, which was driven by credos and manifestos. This freedom led to greater experimentation with new materials and styles. In America during the modern period, practitioners such as Charles and Ray Eames, Eero Saarinen, George Nelson and Florence Knoll became household names.

◄ *Interior of the Farnsworth House, an iconic building designed by architect Mies van der Rohe near Plano, Illinois, between 1945 and 1951.*

Europe

European modernism found its roots predominantly in France and Italy. Faced with the need to rebuild quickly after the Second World War, simple and easy-to-build designs became the go-to style. However, some designers with an Italian and French sense of flair opted for a less austere, sometimes over-the-top aesthetic, with pieces running the gamut from elegant to almost cartoon-like joy. European modernist designers such as Gio Ponti, Ico and Luisa Parisi, Jean Royère and Max Ingrand produced some of the most iconic pieces of modern design.

▸ *Intricate joinery and shaped natural materials feature strongly in many mid-century modern pieces.*

▾ *American Milo Baughman's furniture designs are still popular today for his distinctive but unpretentious style.*

◄ Danish designer Hans J. Wegner's beautiful CH07 Shell chair was designed in 1963.

▼ Sérgio Rodrigues is considered one of the most significant designers of modern Brazilian furniture.

Martin Eisler, Joaquim Tenreiro, Lina Bo Bardi and Oscar Niemeyer are delightfully unique, and often make great statement pieces in a room.

Scandinavia

As if operating in a bubble cut off from the rest of Europe, modernism in Scandinavia developed with little outside interference, so this style is unique and instantly recognizable in the design world. Drawing from the earlier Nordic styles, post-war Scandinavian designers embraced craftsmanship and natural materials – notably teak. They created pieces of timeless design with a sense of elegant utility, of which they were masters. Pieces designed by Finn Juhl, Arne Vodder, Paavo Tynell, Tapio Wirkkala, Nanna Ditzel and Hans J. Wegner are all excellent examples.

South America

Much in the same way as European modernism, there is an elegance associated with many modern pieces from South America. With an abundant supply of exotic woods – most notable at the time was Brazilian rosewood – the designers of this period created some striking pieces to showcase the beautiful figuring and tones of their wood. With a sense of ease, and even a casual demeanour, the pieces produced by designers such as Sérgio Rodrigues, Carlo Hauner and

Japan

Much of modern design finds some influence in traditional Japanese style. Whether it's the austere aesthetic of 1920s Bauhaus or the warmth of 1950s Usonian homes by Frank Lloyd Wright, the concepts behind Japanese architectural aesthetics and the functions of everyday objects were easily adapted to post-war modern design in the West. Emphasizing simplicity and organic

such as Maurice Calka, Günter Beltzig, Verner Panton, Ennio Lucini, Wendell Castle, and collectives like Superstudio created some of the most eye-catching designs of the modern period.

Transitional style

A later interior design idea rather than a modern design movement, transitional style eschews the notion of 'design school' purity and prefers to 'mix it up'. Whether it's the use of Scandinavian style for a Victorian parlour or European minimalism in a barn conversion, the idea is that timeless design can work anywhere. If it's done well, mixing together periods and schools can work beautifully, and you can find many stunning examples.

forms, the designs were meant to be unobtrusive, easy to live and work with. Perhaps the most interesting thing about this style is that, despite being purely modern, each piece pays homage to cultural history. Designers such as Saburo Inui, Isamu Kenmochi and Kenzō Tange, as well as manufacturers such as Tendo Mokko, created exciting, unique new pieces.

Pop modern

Towards the end of the 1950s, Europe was finally getting back on its feet. The war was firmly in the past and a design movement emerged unlike any that had previously existed. With new materials such as plastics and bold new colours becoming available, designers seemed to abandon their manifestos and design ideologies and instead began creating objects that were more like sculpture than furniture. Inspired by Pop art, an irreverent new generation of designers – largely from France, Germany and Italy – produced some outrageous-looking works. Many of these items were little more than style exercises, but designers

A place to rest

The rule of no clutter also applies to the bedroom of a mid-century modern-style home. In a tranquil and efficient Richard Neutra home, for instance, often the only piece of furniture the owner needs to place in the bedroom is a bed. In large mid-century modern homes, the master bedroom will often have its own en-suite bathroom and a separate dressing area with dressing tables and storage. Even in the more modest homes built during this period, such as the tract houses in North America (known colloquially as 'cookie-cutter houses'), the master bedroom would be a separate area for the parents, with full facilities and sometimes a private garden or courtyard area. Pieces such as what is now referred to as the 'Case Study Bed' were common in the mid-century modern home; with its hairpin legs and simple, tilted

headboard, it was perfectly suited to the modern look of the time. Finished with light colours and natural-wood fittings, the mid-century modern-style bedroom is a quiet oasis in the rapidly changing modern world.

▼ A mid-century modern bedroom is light and tranquil. Often there is storage, and a bed with a built-in headboard.

▲ *Bathrooms with colourful floor-to-ceiling tiling became very popular during the mid-century period.*

▶ *This interior designed by Ilse Crawford, using furniture from Swiss company Vitra and Finnish company Artek, includes a sideboard and the Stool 60, both designed by Alvar Aalto.*

A clean approach

As many middle-class people during the mid 20th century were moving out of what was considered the 'dirty city', the bathrooms in the new homes of this period were heavily tiled and even sterile-looking spaces. While new styles and fashions introduced colours such as pink, teal and jade green, the overall preference was for a space that was easy and efficient to use and to keep clean.

When planning to create a mid-century modern-inspired bathroom, one could look to the designs of Frank Lloyd Wright, which are well within the parameters of what is modern. Wright was a master of natural materials and his bathroom designs are a seamless extension of the modern aesthetic seen elsewhere in his work. Using wood, stone and tile, with laminated surfaces in warm hues, a modern bathroom need not look like an operating theatre. The bathroom is a private room, without question, but should be as welcoming as any other room in the home.

The mid-century modern colour palette

The colours of mid-century modern style run the gamut from kitschy and bright tones to a muted and more sophisticated palette. Most of the colours used in this period were pale, but, perhaps surprisingly, bold shades were also popular. When used carefully, these statement colours pack a wonderful design punch. In the uncluttered style of mid-century modern, colour was used to highlight the linear and clean architecture of the period, and provide a backdrop for pieces of art and ceramics. The following introduces the top ten colours of mid-century modern style. These were popular many decades ago and can still work well today.

▲ *Warm and soft browns*

Muted greens

Muted green tones go well with natural woods like teak and walnut and make a welcoming statement in any dining room. Whether used as an accent wall or fully enveloping the room, muted greens can be a restful backdrop that works splendidly with artworks and ceramics. And while a dining room is a good place for these greens, cleverly applied they can serve nicely as an accent colour in the living room or entrance area. Complementary colours for muted greens include gold, browns and darker oranges.

Warm and soft browns

Brown hues were popular in the 1960s and often sparingly used in communal spaces, such as the living room and dining room. Ideally used as an accent wall colour, warm browns work very well as a backdrop for pieces of art and ceramics. If used judiciously, these tones are great in a study or bedroom, and make the perfect companion for lighter woods, such as beech and oak. Warmer browns go well with deeper browns, gold tones and muted greens.

Deep-accent red-brown

Deep-accent browns with a red or purple undertone work well in sophisticated spaces and are considered ideal 'entertaining' colours. Perfectly suited to wood-panelled rooms with leather chairs, deep-accent brown is an alluring tone when used sparingly. Dramatic and bold, these tones are another example of how to use

▲ Muted greens

▲ Deep-accent red-brown

colour to set off modern sculpture and art, and are perfect for highlighting architectural detail in what can be an otherwise simple space. Add bold shades of pink, pale-warm greys and off-whites to create a warm space with a strong presence.

Soft yellows

Soft yellows are a quintessential mid-century modern paint colour that has stood the test of time. While brighter tones can create a sunshiny kitchen or bathroom, more muted hues work wonderfully in dining rooms and entry halls. Muted golds, which were more commonly used in the 1960s, can be used for accent walls, but, unlike the aforementioned colours, do not make an effective backdrop for art and sculptural pieces. Complementary colours to muted yellows include natural wood tones and muted blues.

▲ Soft yellows

▲ Soft blues

Soft blues

Perhaps no colour is more synonymous with 1950s interior design than soft blue. Whether turquoise or aqua, it is a great way to add some fun to the mid-century modern interior. Used in kitchens, bathrooms and children's bedrooms, soft blues can be used as an accent colour or to fill a room. While these tones are not particularly sophisticated, they can be a great backdrop for modern art glass collections. Not many colours work well with soft blues, so keep the accent tone a clean white.

▲ *Muted olives*

▲ *Coral pink*

▲ *Soft and muted orange*

Muted olives

Along the lines of the muted greens, these softer olive tones tend to be lighter and more neutral. A great accent wall colour, muted olive tones are ideal for bedrooms and also work well as a backdrop to photography, ceramics and art. Slightly deeper shades of muted olive also work very well in living rooms and lend an air of elegance in spaces where lighting is limited. Paired with maroon, darker browns and soft blue, this colour can add drama to any space.

Coral pink

This bold tone, ranging from near orange almost to bright pink, is another elemental colour of mid-century modern design. During the 1950s corals were used primarily in kitchens and bathrooms, but today the more muted shades of this colour can be well utilized for an accent wall in bedrooms. When paired with orange it can make a playful and stylish colour scheme for an entryway.

Soft and muted orange

More popular in the 1960s than the 1950s, and a bolder choice when compared to others in the mid-century palette, this colour was often used sparingly for highlighting specific spaces, such as in the kitchen or dining room, or for creating a statement entry door. Many Scandinavian designers of this period used soft oranges to highlight doors and drawers in cabinets and sideboards, which is perhaps why this colour goes so well with teak and walnut, for that glamorous 1960s look.

Greys

It may come as a surprise, but grey was a very popular colour choice during the mid-century modern period. This dark colour makes a bold statement, ideal as an accent wall or a backdrop for brightly coloured art, sculpture and ceramic pieces. While greys were often used in the living rooms of the time, this colour can work well in dining rooms, entryways and bedrooms. When used with olive tones and gold it can create an air of refined elegance.

▲ *Greys*

Warm taupe

Taupe (or beige) was as popular in the mid 20th century as it is today. It was widely used in the mid-century modern home, but was more likely at that time to have a heavy pink undertone. It is easy to brush off taupe as being dull and ubiquitous, but its range is actually quite broad, with undertones that can be easily matched to any accent colour. An easy colour to live with, taupe is a flexible, fail-safe choice.

▲ *Warm taupe*

Mid-century modern woods

The following is an introduction to some of the woods most commonly used in mid-century modern design. By becoming familiar with the various woods and wood veneers that are available, you will be better able to ascertain which would be the most appropriate for your own home.

Afrormosia

While not as common as other woods in modern design, afrormosia was used by designers and manufacturers looking for a versatile and easy material to work with. The wood colour is uniform, with a natural lustre that runs from yellow to medium brown and either a reddish or olive hue. It has a relatively straight, although sometimes interlocking, grain. Afrormosia is often mistaken for teak and is sometimes used as a teak substitute. Native to the African continent, today the afrormosia trade is tightly controlled; the species is listed by CITES (the Convention on International Trade in Endangered Species) as endangered.

▲ *Afrormosia*

Beech

Often used in European modern design – particularly in Scandinavian countries – beech is lightly figured and fairly plain. It is typically a pale cream colour, sometimes with a pink or brown hue. Beech veneer does tend to be slightly darker because the process of slicing the veneer usually requires the wood to be prepared with steam, which gives it a more golden tone. Beech responds well to steaming, bending and lamination, which made it popular with designers such as Bruno Mathsson and Alvar Aalto. Beech is sustainable, widely available and affordable, which makes it a great 'starter' wood for those interested in woodworking.

Cherry

With its pink to reddish brown colouring, and streaks of lighter variation, cherry was very popular with European cabinetmakers during the mid-century modern period. After the Second World War, many designers considered cherry to be a bit of an old-fashioned wood, used mostly for creating little turned curios and jewellery boxes, and perhaps overused in Art Deco furniture design. However, some mid-century modern designers appreciated the straight, even grain and workability of cherry and felt that the wood quite nicely lent itself to the minimal and modern aesthetic. While not CITES listed, the cherry tree is being over-harvested due to its renewed popularity for use as flooring.

▲ *Cherry*

◄ *Beech*

Mahogany

Mahogany is one of the grandes dames of exotic wood in furniture design. With its rich colour, ranging from a pinkish hue to a deep reddish brown, and variegated streaks, for centuries this wood has been popular in finer cabinetry and design. It has a rich lustre, 'chatoyancy' (undulating colours) and a naturally reflective quality that catches and bounces light. Most mahogany pieces will darken with age, which can make it a little difficult to identify older pieces. Mid-century modern mahogany pieces are often veneered. Real South-American mahogany is considered 'vulnerable', but there are various other mahoganies available which are not.

▲ *Mahogany*

Maple

With its pale colouring and fine, even grain figuring, maple is not really a standout wood. It was used as a lining wood by many designers of the post-war period. There was one mid-century modern designer, however, who appreciated the simple beauty of maple and that was American designer Paul McCobb. Many of McCobb's understated pieces were perfectly suited to the wood and are prized by collectors today. One of the more common types of maple in modern design is birdseye maple, which is formed by an aberration that alters the wood's grain, creating a tiny 'swirling' pattern (this was very popular with the Victorians). Maple is considered a sustainable wood.

▲ *Maple*

Oak

Oak was not used very much by modern designers. In fact, by the 1950s oak was considered a bit of a traditional rural wood, therefore not in keeping with the modernist outlook. There are many varieties of oak, but they all have a fairly coarse, open grain and can range in colour from very pale cream to reddish brown. Because of its relatively easy workability (with a pleasant smell when being worked) and ability to take stain well, during the mid-century modern period oak was often 'disguised' to look like other types of wood. Danish designer Hans Wegner enjoyed oak in its natural state, and created many pieces using it. Relatively affordable, oak is a good sustainable wood that is not CITES listed, nor at risk, so this is a guilt-free wood choice.

Brazilian rosewood

There is a sad story to this beautiful wood, which has a dramatic grain figuring and rich colouring that ranges from chocolate-brown to reddish purple streaked with black 'spider webs'. Brazilian rosewood, which had been used for centuries, experienced a resurgence in post-war design, particularly among Scandinavian designers. When the world discovered their designs in the 1950s and 1960s, the demand for Brazilian rosewood skyrocketed, and it was used for many things, from musical instruments to furniture and wall-panelling. By the beginning of the 1970s, the species was facing extinction and shortly thereafter a permanent ban was placed on the harvesting and selling of Brazilian rosewood. Today, it is no longer commercially available and similar woods from other regions such as India, Argentina and Africa are used instead. However, none can match the beauty of the expressive Brazilian rosewood.

▲ *Oak*

▲ *Brazilian rosewood*

Teak

The 1960s as we know them might not have existed without teak; it was the wood of the era. Golden to medium brown in colour, with a straight grain (although it can sometimes be interlocked) and a moderately porous surface, teak is a wood with excellent workability. It is considered the gold standard for durability and decay resistance. One of the finer properties of teak is that the colour will darken to a richer hue as it ages, and darker examples are mistaken for red oak. While it is not CITES listed, and despite most new timber being grown on sustainable plantations worldwide, teak is a very expensive wood.

▲ Teak

▲ Walnut

Walnut

American black walnut is one of the most popular choices for woodworkers in the United States. This versatile, durable wood can range from a pale to dark chocolate brown, or black with a reddish cast. Walnut's grain is as varied as its colour; sometimes tight and straight, other times very interlocked and burled. In the post-war period, walnut found favour with a new group of artisans who were reclaiming the traditions of the American craft movement, reinventing it with a modern aesthetic. Some master craftsmen, such as George Nakashima, Phillip Lloyd Powell and Sam Maloof, favoured walnut. It was also the first choice of designer Vladimir Kagan. A beautifully lustrous wood, walnut is a sustainable choice.

Zebrawood

One of the most recognizable woods is the distinctive zebrawood. It has a light-brown colour with dark, almost black streaks, which form the stripes that give it its name. It has a coarse texture and busy grain. Zebrawood is a dense wood that is not the easiest to work with, but it is favoured for its looks. While not as expensive as other exotic woods, zebrawood is still pricey. It is not CITES listed, but it is considered to be at risk.

▲ Zebrawood

▲ Afrormosia

▲ Beech

▲ Cherry

▲ Mahogany

▲ Maple

▲ Oak

▲ Brazilian rosewood

▲ Teak

▲ Walnut

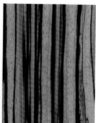

▲ Zebrawood

Choosing the right pieces for your lifestyle

With the wide range of mid-century modern designs available, it might seem a daunting task to choose the right pieces for your home. Beyond the fact that you want to enjoy the way it looks, you may have other demands, for example if you have children or regular guests. Making the right choice is therefore often a matter of compromise. Mid-century modern design will have a practical and attractive solution for most problems. Designers and architects of this period were all about creating design solutions and they left a legacy of pieces well suited to individual needs. Choosing the right pieces will make your life a little easier and add a stylish look to your home.

Storage for families

It is not always easy choosing design objects and accessories for your home, and this is made more challenging when there are children to consider. The needs of the busy family are many and most choose to be more pragmatic with home décor rather than stylish. However, there are several mid-century modern options that will work very well with the day-to-day life of the busy family. Storage and organization is key when it comes to keeping family life together in the mid-century modern home. Architects of the period often designed family homes with plenty of built-in storage, including in the entrance hall, bathroom and living room.

► *The Arne Vodder model 211 sideboard with distinctive coloured drawers.*

Besides this, one of the easiest ways to add storage to any room is with a sideboard. Versatile, practical and attractive, it is astonishing that these wonderful pieces of furniture fell out of fashion. Often designed for the dining room, most sideboards have drawers as well as cupboard space and are available in many sizes. Even a sideboard in the hallway, if space allows, will control clutter and help to keep the many things children need organized. The Scandinavians are the masters of sideboards and while some can be pricey, many are very affordable.

Built to last

Another consideration for family living is durability. Here's where you may want to avoid the lighter designs of Scandinavian chairs and sofas, not

▲ The mid-century modern style can offer practical and stylish design solutions for a young family.

because these pieces aren't sturdy and well made, but they might not be able to take a daily dose of rambunctious children. American mid-century modern pieces can be more helpful for this. Solid pieces that are often lower to the floor, such as those designed by Adrian Pearsall and Edward Wormley, were very much designed with the family in mind. You can find these pieces for very reasonable prices and, while some may need to be freshened up with new upholstery, they are a sensible investment that will last until after the kids have left home.

The gracious host

If you're a person who has frequent guests around, you may want to consider a daybed. In the 1950s and 1960s almost every mid-century modern designer created their own take on this piece of furniture. Some of these are simple fold-down models; others are a basic platform that becomes a bed when the back cushions are removed; some unfold in complex ways, revealing, as well as the bed itself, a side table and storage. Daybeds are more popular in Europe than North America, but can be found pretty much everywhere. Most online auction houses, particularly the Scandinavian ones, offer wonderful daybeds at very reasonable prices. The daybed can be slipped into almost any room of the home, particularly a home office. A well-designed mid-century modern daybed will offer your guests a comfortable and smart place to spend the night.

Entertaining in style

A coat rack is a common feature of mid-century modern style. Placed in the entrance hall, it offers an elegant solution to the problem of where to put all those guests' coats. Another indispensable aspect of mid-century modern entertaining was the home cocktail party, and there was no shortage of designs that made entertaining easy and elegant. The idea may seem a little silly in the contemporary home, but a home cocktail cabinet can be a bold statement piece, and useful for those who enjoy a good drink with close friends. Cocktail cabinets are ideal for storing all the accoutrements, such as bottles, shakers and glassware. There are essentially two styles: the elegant teak and rosewood bars made in the Scandinavian countries and the occasionally outrageous designs of the bars made in Italy. Whatever your choice, they are often affordable and can be a unique piece within your mid-century modern design scheme.

Additional seating and occasional tables

Those who like to entertain will often have a need for extra seating and surfaces. There are several styles of mid-century modern stools to suit your needs and personal style preference. Small stools are compact, such as the 'Tulip', designed by Eero Saarinen, so can easily be put in storage and brought out when needed, or left in the space and kept to the side. Stools are great not only for guests but also children, who can use them for working on crafts, homework or just watching TV.

Nesting tables are a great solution for creating extra surfaces when needed. These small tables stack – or nest – together into a discreet and compact side table.

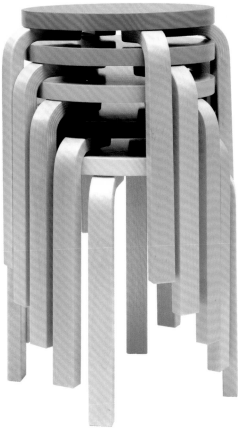

▲ *Alvar Aalto's stackable stools are produced by Artek and come in a variety of attractive colours.*

◄ *A bar trolley may seem old-fashioned today, but it does provide an opportunity to display some classic mid-century modern pieces.*

Quality versus price

Mid-century modern style has never been more popular, and with this resurgence has come, rather inevitably, the copies. Many supposedly reputable companies and big-name designers profit quite handsomely by replicating modern design pieces with low production costs, selling 'mid-century modern' furniture and accessories. Many consumers are not aware the item they are purchasing is a plagiarized copy of a known design and, in some cases, the item – often made cheaply – is one of poor quality that will not last.

You get what you pay for

The main argument against buying an original always seems to come down to price. True, a lot of these designs are expensive, but they are also well made, guaranteed and will become a family heirloom, whereas the cheap copy will soon become valueless. A generation ago, household furnishings were expected to be of good quality, well made and built to endure the rigours of family life. Today, with inexpensive flat-pack dominating the consumer landscape, long-lasting quality is no longer an expectation. With such a short lifespan, there is no need to think of build quality. Rather sadly, furniture has become like fashion: an ephemeral part of our lives.

A worthwhile investment

When mid-century modern first became popular, there were many places one could go to find well-made period pieces of furniture that were often cheaper than their flat-pack counterparts. Whether at flea markets, car-boot sales or charity shops, it was possible to find a mid-century modern chair that, with a bit of sprucing up, would work in the home. The belief was simply that if a chair had already lasted fifty years, it would last fifty more. For fans of mid-century modern style, this was not only economical but also a sensible ecological choice. Finding a great old piece of modern design saved it from the landfill and eased the environmental burden of a newly produced item. Today the mid-century modern look has become popular, and finding quality pieces has become a little more difficult. However, with a bit of rewarding effort you will not

▲ *An original Adrian Pearsall chair, model 1404-C, designed for Craft Associates, reupholstered in Knoll Hourglass fabric.*

only have achieved the mid-century modern look and experience, you will have made a great investment; many classic modern design pieces continue to increase in value.

Mass-market modern

If design icons are out of your price range, there are other options. Not every piece of furniture produced in the mid 20th century was a 'classic' or an 'icon' of design. Most pieces were what's known today as 'mass-market modern', for the greater buying public. Companies such as Broyhill, Stanley and Lane in the United States, Dux of Denmark and Pastoe of the Netherlands all made good, reasonably priced furniture in large quantities, making it affordable to collectors today.

If you happen to have a penchant for Danish Modern but perhaps find it too costly for your budget, look for items of the same period that were made in Sweden or Norway. It's a fact of Scandinavian design that the 'Made in Denmark' label carries a premium, but pieces made in the neighbouring countries have the same style and are often much more affordable.

▼ A stylish set of two No. 983-103 t-back lounge chairs, designed by Milo Baughman for Thayer Coggin in the 1970s.

Selecting a quality piece

A long-standing design credo is that each room deserves at least one quality item, and the mid-century modern room is no different. It's easy to learn how to tell a quality item. Certainly there were manufacturers of the period whose brand meant quality – Cassina, Fontana Arte, Knoll, Herman Miller and Singer & Sons are names that assure quality. But of course, these names will always come at a premium. Here are a few things to look out for when selecting a piece of furniture:

▷ On wooden-framed pieces, such as shelving and seating, always look at the joinery – i.e. where the pieces of wood are joined. Clean and sculpted or curved seams are an easy indicator of build quality. A seam that has opened slightly does not necessarily mean poor quality, as changes in humidity and temperature can cause this to happen on the best of pieces, and an open joinery seam on a quality piece often has an easy remedy.

▷ Better-quality pieces rarely have visible screws, or visible screw covers, holding the item together – particularly with chairs and sofas.

A piece made from solid wood is generally an indicator of quality, but many high-end design pieces are veneered.

▷ When it comes to cabinetry, such as sideboards and storage units, a finished back is a good indicator of quality. Also, well-made cabinetry will often be finished with a 'lesser wood' on the inside, usually maple.

▷ Knowing about the various woods of the period can be a simple way to quickly determine quality. Teak, rosewood and walnut were the top three used by designers of the period and are the easiest to learn how to spot. Should you happen upon a sofa framed in teak there's a good chance it's going to be a quality piece.

▷ A well-made piece should be solid and even the most delicate-seeming of Scandinavian designs will be well planted and not shaky or wobbly.

▷ On Danish furniture there is sometimes a 'Danish Furniture Makers Control' sticker or badge. Almost any piece with this badge will be one of quality.

▶ *Charles and Ray Eames were the pioneers of single-shell moulded chairs. Their first successful design was realized in 1950. This style has since been replicated by many manufacturers.*

▶▶ *Finn Juhl's designs are a fine example of Danish modern. Many are still in production.*

How not to live in a mid-century modern museum

One of the most common pitfalls when trying to achieve a mid-century modern space is that, whether intentionally or not, some homes end up looking like a time capsule of mid-century life. While this may seem charming – or at least academically intriguing – the effect is, more often than not, an unwelcoming one. An appreciation of mid-century modern design and contemporary living are not mutually exclusive concepts.

▲ *When planning your mid-century modern home, avoid inundating spaces with your collection of period objects.*

What about technology?

There seems to be a philosophy in all design styles of 'hiding the tech'. Televisions get hidden in cabinets and sound systems are tucked away in cupboards. This is unnecessary and a waste of storage space. A room should feel welcoming and one of the easiest ways to achieve this is by demonstrating that the room is lived in and enjoyed. A TV is not just a large, black rectangle; it is proof that people use and enjoy the room. However, as with all things, one must strike a sensible balance. Be aware of anything that may take away from the calm, clutter-free aspect of modern design: for example, invest in some cable organizers and a DVD storage cabinet. One good idea for organizing the home entertainment area is to have a period sideboard or credenza. These low storage cabinets can be used to hold a TV and come with additional storage space beneath for DVDs, music and technology. The look will be contemporary, but will work well in a mid-century modern space.

Curate your collection

Many people come to appreciate mid-century modern design through collecting. Often it can start as a simple penchant for period ceramics, old technology like transistor radios, or any interesting object of the time. Many collectors are quite rightly pleased with their items and wish to display them. However, this can lead to a veritable inundation of objects. Let's say, for instance, you are a collector of art glass and wish to place some of these items

on display. A few pieces on a shelf or side table can add colour and charm to any room, but if you place hundreds of them on a shelf the effect is overwhelming and can even be disconcerting. Choosing to display just a few objects from your collection gives each piece breathing space and permits you and your visitors to properly appreciate them. If you are a collector with several examples, it is a good idea to rotate what is displayed. Doing so will help to refresh the look of the room.

▲ *Today, the television is part of everyday life, so you should not feel obliged to hide it away.*

Embrace the new

Old stereos and televisions have a nostalgic charm, but, unlike a well-designed mid-century modern sofa, their function does not endure. A delightful old refrigerator may still keep your food cold but is far from energy efficient. Architects and designers of the 1950s and 1960s embraced new materials and technologies, and probably would have loved the idea of a wall-mounted flat-screen TV and wireless music playback. Mixing older designs with newer items can work quite well and makes life a bit more convenient.

Reflecting your personal style

Because there is so much variety in the different styles of mid-century modern design, there is something to reflect most individual personal styles and tastes. Maybe you prefer the clean and elegant lines of a Florence Knoll sideboard, or the sensually sculpted forms of a Vladimir Kagan chair. Personal taste is not a measurable variable; it simply comes down to how you feel about a given item of mid-century modern design and how it will fit with your day-to-day life. You may find yourself perusing a local flea market and stumble upon a mid-century modern vase of relatively low value, but if that vase appeals to you in some way, if it simply makes you smile, then what better reason for it to be in your home? The act of personalizing your space should tell a story, and that is the story of you. Simply take your time, learn how to discern a quality piece and the story of you, at least the home décor aspect of it, will begin to unfold.

Fill in the missing pieces

If you are new to mid-century modern design and wish to begin incorporating it into your home décor, it is always best to start with pieces that are missing from your current design scheme. For example, if you're in need of a coffee table, try scouting out the local antiques and speciality dealers for a period piece. You will often be able to find a mid-century modern coffee table for a good price (and for less than a new one) that will not only fit well with your home and lifestyle but will undoubtedly be of a finer material, such as teak or walnut, and of a higher build quality. Take time to visit various dealers and online sales before making a choice. To reflect your personal style, objects should bring you some joy as well as serving a purpose.

Mix it up

Once you start 'filling in the gaps', while furnishing your home with quality items of furniture, you will

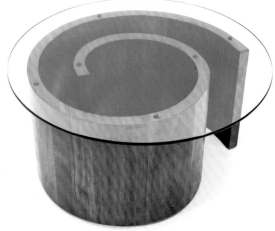

▶ *Mid-century modern design incorporates such a variety of styles that there is something to reflect everyone's taste. This spiral 'snail' coffee table can support different sizes of glass tops to perfectly suit your space.*

begin to see your own mid-century modern taste emerge. You may find yourself leaning towards the fluid and clean lines of Scandinavian style or the linear elegance of European minimalism – whatever the style you prefer, you can now begin replacing items. And this is where you can start creating a cohesive and relaxing look for your home. Never be afraid to 'mix it up' when it comes to choosing mid-century modern pieces; a sofa from the 1960s can work quite well with a chair from the 1940s. The idea is not to replicate a home from the 1950s or 1960s, but rather to create a home with mid-century modern pieces that is inviting to others and comfortable for you.

▲ *This 17th-century property has been given a mid-century modern feel by removing walls to create an open-plan space. Carefully chosen mid-century pieces, such as the Bertoia High Back Bird Chair and Ottoman have been mixed with other items that reveal the owner's personal tastes.*

◄ If you have a period property with original features, such as a fireplace, introduce a mid-century modern twist to the room with carefully chosen accessories.

▼ A sideboard can provide an ideal space to showcase your collection.

Accessorize

One of the best, and most affordable, ways to reflect your own personal style with mid-century modern design is through accessories. From lighting to books to ceramics, a few carefully chosen items on your tables and shelves will speak volumes. Glasswork can add a flash of colour and can draw the eye to a particular area of the space that you may feel worthy of attention. Books are a timeless way of livening up a room,

but books for the sake of decoration is never a good way to go. If you opt for accessorizing with books, make sure they are books you know and enjoy. Ceramics, whether colourful or muted and neutral, lend a wonderfully grounding effect to a space. The natural material of ceramic pieces from the mid-century modern period can work with any room: larger pieces can fill a bare floor space, while smaller ones can add a finishing touch to a mantel or shelf.

When it comes to accessorizing, a good rule is moderation. Never clutter or fill the space with hundreds of little objects. The effect is overwhelming and the collection cannot be appreciated. Another good rule is not to line every surface with objects: a shelf lined with perfectly spaced ceramic pieces, for instance, looks forced and frankly amateurish. The best way is to cluster the pieces. If you have a mantel, put a few well-selected accessories towards one side of it. This will give a more dynamic and interesting appearance. The same is true of shelving and tables – a 'forced' look will always show its hand, whereas a well-curated and well-placed collection will be the best testament to your own style.

Adding sentimental value

Personal effects and family heirlooms are a wonderful way of individualizing a space.

When looking at old photos of homes of the mid-century modern period it is not uncommon to see an antique chair or a family quilt placed over the back of a modern lounge chair. If you have items of sentimental value, do not worry that they are not of the mid-century modern time frame, as with careful placement these items can mix quite happily with newer antiques.

▼ *Wall dividers are useful for displaying accessories across an entire wall.*

3. A ROOM-BY-ROOM GUIDE

ENTERING

The entryway

The entryway of any home should be an invitation – warm and welcoming – but it should also be organized and functional. There should be space for coming and going, some last-minute preening before leaving, and a place to sit and take off shoes and boots upon returning. There should be a place to keep coats and jackets, and a spot to toss keys and post. In the mid-century modern home, the era of the home cocktail party and ladies' socials, first impressions were very important, and so the details of the entryway were given close attention. While such social functions may appear outdated today, the idea of an efficient, thoughtful entryway remains important.

Seating

Generally, an entryway will need a place to sit, and the approach taken by many architects of the period was to provide built-in seating. As time passed, and the idea of an open-plan space became the norm, built-ins became less popular. An alternative to the built-in bench is a stand-alone one, many of which were produced during the mid-century modern period. As well as seating, many of these designs offer storage to keep the area clutter-free. Some include an integrated planter or space for displaying items.

There are many varieties of mid-century modern bench. They come in various different sizes and range from the very high-end, such as those designed by Finn Juhl and Vladimir Kagan, to the mass-market ones produced by American manufacturers. If budget and space are an issue, a simple solution can be repurposing a period phone bench. Phone benches are abundant, inexpensive, and work very well in an entryway.

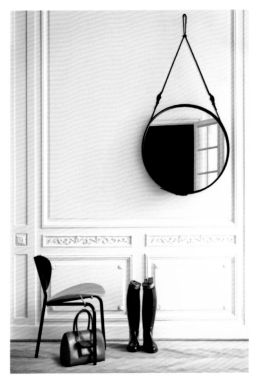

▲ *The most successful entryways are often those that are kept as simple as possible with only one or two items of furniture and minimal accessories.*

▶ *With their Hang-It-All wall-mounted coat rack, American designers Charles and Ray Eames brought an element of fun to an everyday object. Originally multicoloured, American company Herman Miller now produce the design in a variety of separate colours.*

▶ *Plants offer a delightful welcome to any home, but be careful not to overwhelm the space.*

Lighting

It may not be something you can design for a space, but there are options available for bringing natural lighting into the entry space. Natural lighting allows for plants and will cut down on the need to use task lighting. A relatively easy and inexpensive way to introduce natural light to your hallway is to use a front door that has built-in windows – but make sure the door you choose is suitable for weather and climate.

People are often surprised to learn that many mid-century modern homes had recessed pocket lighting. Many modern homes in the 1950s and 1960s utilized these fittings, and they are just as popular today. If your home is in need of better lighting and you want to incorporate a mid-century

modern style, recessed pocket lights are an excellent way to go.

Planters and plants

Plants featured heavily in the entryways of mid-century modern homes. In fact, some architects at the time designed permanent planters for the floor of the entrance. While few may have that option today, there are many inexpensive planters available that will suit. The trick to plants in the entryway is to keep it simple and stick to a single variety of plant; do not overwhelm what is likely to be a small space.

There are many great mid-century modern planters available, ranging from built-in versions on benches to the simple elegance of those created by companies such as Architectural Pottery. Whatever option you choose, it is always best to keep it simple and scaled appropriately for the space.

Wood panelling

A design signature of many architects from the this period is wood panelling. This can work well in any room, including the entryway. There are many panelling options available today, but most are synthetic and best avoided. The most cost-effective way of getting a real wood-panelled wall look is to use faced plywood. Available in large sheets, and veneered with real wood, these work quite well. Try walnut, which was the preferred wood choice of the mid-century modern era.

Carpets and rugs

A simple way of adding colour and texture to the entrance is to add a carpet. It need not be a period one, seeing as few from the 1950s and 1960s survive in good shape today. Carpets in the mid-century modern style can be found at most major retailers and online sellers. Quality materials, such as wool, are not only decorative but also surprisingly tough and stain-resistant. If your hallway will see a great deal of people traffic, materials like jute and seagrass offer a natural solution and are incredibly durable options for an entry rug.

Additional elements

Another key piece that will help make a practical and efficient entrance is a wall mirror, of which you will find a rich abundance from the mid-century modern period, in various shapes and sizes. Add to this a coat stand for your guests' belongings, and an elegant clock, and you have the elements of a smart and functional mid-century modern entryway.

▼ *If you have a large space, a long bench or sofa with built-in side table can be really useful in an entryway.*

Case study

Designer Amy Lau > **Year** 2016 > **Place** East Hampton, New York State

The entrance to a home of any period should always be welcoming and relaxing. As the saying goes, there should be a place for everything and everything in its place. A cluttered and disorderly entrance sets a negative tone, but this is an easy problem to fix.

Architects of the mid-century modern period were always experimenting with residential design. They studied how people lived and how they used the spaces in which they lived. The belief was that better living could be achieved through design. To this end, the entrance was given a great deal of attention. It was not simply a 'mud room' but the starting point for the well-designed life.

Consider the elegant entrance of this home. Everything about the design of this entry area works splendidly. The simplicity and restraint of the design objects used demonstrate a 'less is more' approach, where nothing unnecessary is added. The colour palette, with the bright red vase and blue storage with coordinating yellow panels, is stimulating without being overpowering. Bench seating, a staple of the mid-century modern entryway, provides somewhere to sit while you remove your shoes, and a row of abstract artworks pick up some of the colours from the shelving unit.

Entry bench *With the use of this long, slatted bench, there is plenty of seating space as well as a surface to drop items temporarily when you first enter the house. Ordinarily, such a long bench might detract from a space, but this one actually elongates the room, with the slats running in the same direction as the entryway itself.*

Lighting *There are task lights in abundance in this entryway, spaced evenly to distribute light along the length of the room, but it is the natural light flooding in through the full-height glass front door which helps to make this entryway feel so spacious.*

Rug *Like the slats of the bench, the herringbone weave of this rug runs in the same direction as the longest wall of the entryway. Rugs like this one, woven from natural materials, are a common feature of a mid-century modern entrance hall.*

Storage *No mid-century modern entryway is complete without an attractive storage unit, designed to display a collection of books or carefully chosen accessories while also keeping everyday objects, such as shoes or door keys, out of sight.*

Signature colours

It cannot be overstated how important the entryway is to the overall feel and tone of a home. A claustrophobic and chaotic space is simply not the kind of greeting your visitors should expect. Accents and carefully selected colours make all the difference here. Often the best approach is to use a softer, muted background tone, which is then accented with pops of colour for character and interest.

This entryway is almost entirely creams and browns, but it feels quite lively. The two main components of this space are the flood of natural light through the large window and the colourful red door. When using neutral colours in the background, there is often a tendency to keep the accents the same. While this can be effective in some minimalist spaces, it can be a little cold for an entryway. Adding a few well-chosen, colourful items will bring a spark to the entryway and create a welcoming home.

In this entryway colour has also been introduced through the array of plants on display. Lighting is a source of colour that is often overlooked, but here the natural light that pours through the large windows creates a warm glow. against the warm brown-and-red colour scheme.

F-508 Peanut Planter

The ceramic works of Architectural Pottery, a Los Angeles company founded by Max and Rita Lawrence in 1950, appear in many mid-century modern period photos, and are icons in their own right. The company was so successful in its forward-thinking approach that its works were exhibited at MoMA only a year after it was founded. In 1998, VesseL USA Inc. reintroduced several of these pieces, many designed by LaGardo Tackett. Each of these pieces is true to its original, timeless design.

Architectural Pottery designs were very much reflective of modernist ideas: that good design can be applied to all aspects of modern life, and that all consumer objects could be improved upon to make life better. If one of the primary goals of mid-century modern design was cohesiveness, this pottery was a huge success. One could take any of the various styles of Architectural Pottery, display them together, and they will work. The design across the range, while varied in shape and size, is extremely cohesive.

VesseL USA Inc. was founded in 1998 to revive the stunningly simple planters and ceramic designs from the Architectural Pottery Collection. The F-508 Peanut Planter comes with a walnut base. Fibreglass makes this large piece easier to move into position once it is filled. Where space allows, it would work beautifully in an entryway. Alternatively, an optional drain hole may be added for outdoor use.

Designer
John Follis for Architectural Pottery

Manufacturer
VesseL USA Inc.

Year
1950s

Place
USA

Materials
Fibreglass, wood

Dimensions
Length: 152.5 cm
Width: 35.5 cm
Height: 5 cm

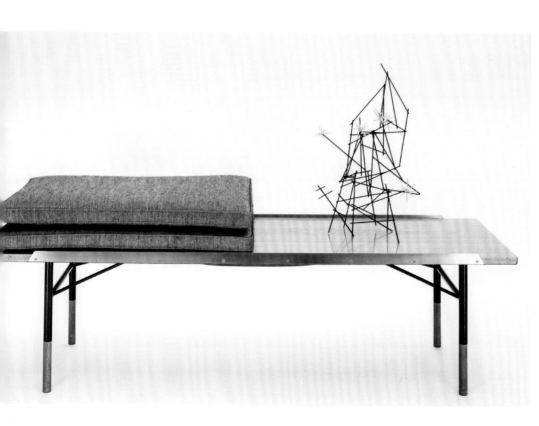

Model BO 101 bench

Almost every designer of the mid-century modern period designed a bench at some point in their career. The bench was seen as a practical addition to almost any space, whether as a functional part of an entryway, a convenient place at the foot of a bed, or even to be taken outside and enjoyed in the sun. Examples include the wooden slatted George Nelson bench (still produced in the United States by Herman Miller) and the small, delicate upholstered bench made by Jens Risom. Whatever the choice, good seating in the entrance was considered requisite.

One of the most beautiful of these benches was the Model BO 101 bench, designed by Finn Juhl and manufactured by Bovirke of Denmark in 1952. A simple teak platform framed with brass accents is supported by a solid steel frame. It was a sturdy piece, despite its delicate appearance. One of the reasons this bench is a cut above the rest is its versatility. With the addition of cushions, it serves well as a bench, but remove the cushions and it can double as a coffee table. Finn Juhl is known for having created some of the most beautiful objects in design history. His chairs are, quite simply, among the finest ever designed. This bench easily demonstrates how practical can also be beautiful.

Designer
Finn Juhl

Manufacturer
Bovirke

Year
1952

Place
Denmark

Materials
Teak, brass, metal

Dimensions
(Large model)
Length: 225 cm
Depth:45 cm
Height: 39 cm

Sunflower clock

It is an enduring practice to include a decorative clock in the entryway of mid-century modern homes. Architects often chose to design the space to accommodate a built-in wall clock, while others trusted the homeowner to install a suitable timepiece to complement the style of their furniture and fittings. Generally speaking, entryway clocks were elegant, sometimes cased in wood, and probably a little oversized.

One of the most prolific creators of clock designs was the famous agency George Nelson & Associates, and the Sunflower clock is one of their most successful designs. From the late 1940s onwards, George Nelson was commissioned by the Howard Miller Clock Company to create a line of modern clocks that did not require a serious amount of expensive retooling between each separate model. What was initially intended as a short collaboration stretched to thirty-five years, with George Nelson and his team of designers creating more than 150 clock designs in an array of shapes, sizes and materials. The well-known Sunflower clock, designed by Irving Harper, is still popular and collectable.

Another fine example of a George Nelson & Associates collaboration is the Ball clock, also designed by Irving Harper. Many variants were produced over the years, making it the most ubiquitous model seen in design-conscious homes today.

Designer
Irving Harper for George Nelson & Associates

Manufacturer
Originally the Howard Miller Clock Company, today produced by Vitra

Year
1958

Place
USA

Materials
Birch plywood, lacquered metal, high-grade quartz

Dimensions
Diameter: 75 cm
Depth: 7.5 cm

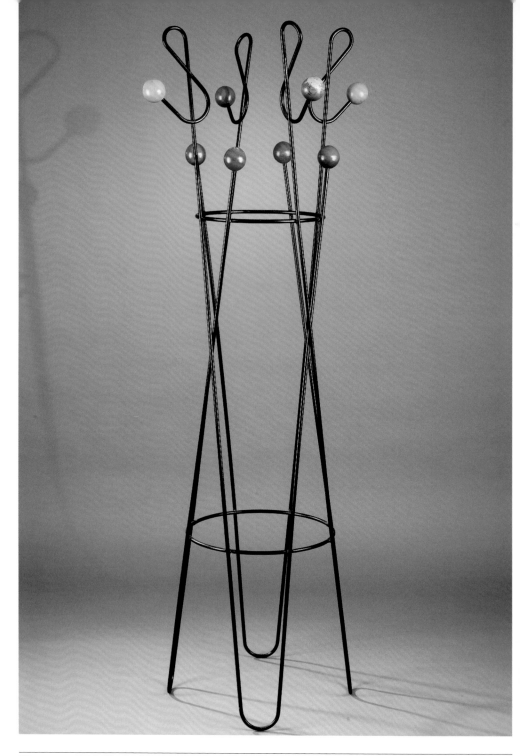

Clé de Sol coat rack

It is often a running joke in television sitcoms and films that when someone throws a house party, the guests' coats ended up in a pile on the parents' bed. While many entryways have built-in storage, the space will usually be filled with the items belonging to the family, leaving little or no room for the coats and jackets of visitors. A great solution for temporary storage of your guests' outerwear is the coat rack, and there are numerous mid-century modern styles to choose from. Somewhat surprisingly, coat racks are more popular (and therefore more expensive) in Europe than they are in North America.

The most distinctive coat rack designs in the mid-century modern style are the steel stands of French designer Roger Feraud. Born in 1890, Feraud was an innovative designer who welcomed the use of new materials, creating playful and bold pieces, produced mostly through his partnership with the French company Cromos. Feraud's pieces were often fun for the sake of it, and this carefree philosophy can easily be seen in his coat rack designs. The Clé de Sol is a typical example of his work, made from enamelled steel with colourful wooden balls. His coat racks have a unique quality often found in French designs from the mid-century modern period. Whether it's a place to dry your umbrella after walking home in the rain, a place to store your shoulder bag, or simply a way of keeping house guests out of your bedroom, a coat rack is a good idea.

Designer
Roger Feraud

Manufacturer
GEO

Year
1950s

Place
France

Materials
Painted wood, enamelled steel

Dimensions
Height: 178 cm
Diameter: 64 cm

Model JH 501 armchair

With its key feature of an elegantly curved back formed from a single piece of shaped wood, Hans J. Wegner's Model JH 501 armchair, usually referred to as 'The Chair', became the designer's calling card to the rest of the design world when it first appeared in the late 1940s. Indeed, the chair helped to introduce the world to the emerging talents of Scandinavian designers and architects and put Danish modernism on the cultural map.

Although the chair is a relatively simple design, the forming of the back piece and the discreetly curved seat are a masterpiece of organic functionality. All evidence of joinery is cleverly hidden; the back and arms are carved from a single piece of wood, creating the overall effect of seamless flow throughout the construction.

Although Wegner produced over 400 designs for chairs in his life, 'The Chair' is arguably his best known work, in part because of its appearance on stage during the first televised election debate between John F. Kennedy and Richard Nixon on October 1960. Viewers across America inundated TV stations after the broadcast to ask for information about where they could buy the chairs.

Designer
Hans J. Wegner

Manufacturer
Johannes Hansen

Year
1949

Place
Denmark

Materials
Teak, leather

Dimensions
Total height: 70 cm
Width: 63 cm
Depth: 52 cm

RELAXING

The living room

The living room of any home is where one's style is put on full display. Unlike the utilitarian needs of the kitchen, or the private spaces of the bedroom, the living room is where we often entertain both friends and strangers alike. Like the entrance, it must be well organized and inviting.

There are several elements that make up a successful living room design, and one of the most important is good, comfortable seating. In a culture that too often equates comfort with excessive padding, it is incorrectly believed that the simple designs of mid-century modern seating cannot be comfortable. To those new to mid-century modern design, it can come as a surprise to experience just how comfortable many of these period pieces are.

But there is more to creating a comfortable and inviting living room than signature pieces of furniture. The use of neutral tones, natural materials, task lighting and a considerate arrangement of furniture all help in the creation of a comfortable space in which people enjoy spending time.

▲ When it was presented in 1949, Finn Juhl's Chieftain Chair was an innovation in Danish furniture design. This piece is inspired by the contemporary art scene of the time as well as art and tools from ancient cultures. It may not look it, but it is surprisingly comfortable.

▶ Nils Strinning's String shelf system was designed in 1949 and has become a classic example of Scandinavian mid-century modern style. The modular shelving is lightweight but stable. It is simple to assemble and the shelves can be easily repositioned to suit any space.

Organization

If there is one core maxim at the heart of the mid-century modern living room, it is organization. Multifunctional pieces were engineered to make life easy and free from clutter. Modular wall units and storage systems offered homeowners a way of displaying select items from their collections, while cupboards stored the necessities of daily living. Wall-mounted modular wall units cleared up floor space and could be added to if more shelving or storage was needed.

One of the most popular shelving systems of the period was the modular, wall-mounted Royal

System®, designed by Poul Cadovius of Denmark in 1958. Produced in great numbers, it is easy to find at reasonable prices. Other modular systems of the time were George Nelson's shelving unit, the Comprehensive Storage System (CSS), Nils Strinning's String shelf system and the wall units of Finn Juhl. All are worth exploring.

Even coffee tables, particularly those of the American designers, were often cleverly designed to incorporate drawers, magazine racks and even coffee-pot warmers. The idea was to promote relaxation through purposeful efficiency.

Lighting

Lighting in the living room is incredibly important and must be carefully considered. The objective of living-room lighting is to create a mood. Choosing the correct lighting is more often a matter of personal taste than it is a steadfast rule, but you will want to avoid harsh, cold lighting.

One of the interesting aspects of many lamps manufactured during the 1950s and 1960s is that they were designed to be fitted with the old, clear (not frosted) incandescent light bulbs. A clear light bulb casts a very defined shadow, and many designers in the mid 20th century worked with this attribute, designing lamps and shades that would cast wonderful shadows onto the wall and ceiling, and lend an element of visual texture to the space. For example, Finnish designer Tapio Wirkkala, the man who, it is said, 'illuminated Finland', designed numerous lamps with shades specifically designed to create intricate shadows on the ceiling and walls. Today, if you wish to create the same shadow-and-light effect, you can do so with the use of clear, energy-efficient LED bulbs, which have the advantage of lasting much longer and remaining cool.

The general rule when it comes to illuminating the living space is to use soft task lighting, such as side-table lamps, a good reading floor lamp or broad task lighting, to accompany overhead recessed spot lights. As with colour, lighting in any space must be experimented with until the right balance is achieved. You should aim to highlight key areas of the room, showcase key pieces of a personal collection and ensure there is sufficient light when needed for working or reading.

A quiet corner

In the mid-century modern living room, there was always a quiet corner with a comfortable lounge chair and a lamp designed to read by. There are many lamps from this period throughout the world that were designed to illuminate the corners of living rooms. The preferred lamp was the floor lamp, which could often be adjusted to suit the reader. Floor lamps have fallen out of fashion in recent years, but given the number of styles made during the 1950s and 1960s, they deserve consideration.

Technology

These days, unlike the 1950s and 1960s, there is much more in the way of new technology to deal with in the living room. As well as being places where people can entertain in a calm, relaxing environment, the living rooms of today need to be flexible to cater for multimedia technologies. While there is a tendency among many, when designing a living room, to 'hide the tech', it should be remembered that architects and designers of the mid-century modern period loved new technology, and would probably have welcomed the wall-mounted flat-screen TV as a replacement for the heavy, clunky televisions of the time.

The idea of wireless music playback through an MP3 player dock would have been embraced by post-war designers, who often experimented with technology and welcomed the new. So should you!

Valuable storage space is lost to the idea that a flat-screen TV is something that should be ashamedly tucked away in a cabinet or cupboard. However, the TV should not compete for attention in the space. For example, it is inadvisable to put one above the fireplace because this will distract from this wonderful feature. A solution for a free-standing TV is to place it on a sideboard, which offers plenty of storage inside.

Older stereo technology can work in a contemporary living room space, if you have room for it. Many claim that older stereo technology, particularly from high-end brands, sounds better than most new equipment. An easy way of updating audio equipment is through a wireless device, which can be fitted to older audio equipment and, when selected, will allow playback from any wireless device, such as a phone or laptop. However, do not overwhelm the living room space; as always, keep it simple and clean.

▲ A collection of Arne Jacobsen Swan and Egg chairs in the living area of the Ahm House in Hertfordshire, England, designed by Jørn Utzon and Povl Ahm.

Stone

The use of stone was popular during the mid-century modern period. Architects Eliot Noyes and Marcel Breuer were masters at incorporating local stone into their designs, creating homes that were at one with their environment. Building a fireplace surround might be more than most are willing to take on, but there are other options for working with stone. Stone elements are now engineered that can be easily and affordably installed as flooring. Wall tiles are also manufactured with engineered stone to create the look of real stone. Avoid anything that immediately looks fake and opt for quality. Mid-century modern is about timelessness and that is always best achieved through quality materials.

Case study

Owner(s) Mark Neely and Paul Kefalides > **Year(s)** 2013 > **Place** San Rafael, California, USA

This living room in an original, almost untouched Joseph Eichler home ticks pretty much every box when it comes to creating a wonderful mid-century modern space. It uses a combination of carefully collected period classics from around the world such as a Hans Wegner Sawback chair, a DF-2000 cabinet by Raymond Loewy and a light designed by Greta Von Nessen, to achieve a timeless mid-century modern look.

Other features that work well here include the abundant use of natural materials, such as the marvellous stonework of the fireplace surround, the neutral fabric of the seating and the wood and marble coffee table. They offer warmth and a wonderfully tactile experience that should be the goal of anyone looking to create an inviting mid-century modern space. What also makes this space so successful is the inclusion of small personal details: for example, the cluster of objects on the coffee table.

The mid-century modern living room is a place of private respite as well as social engagement. It is important for the room to be balanced in terms of materials, colours and design objects. In this living room we see a place where people can easily and comfortably sit around and chat, but also simply relax alone and enjoy the fire.

Mid-Century Modern at Home

Natural light *Task lighting for specific areas of a living room is always important, but the use of as much natural light as possible will add to the overall sense of space. Full-height windows also enhance the feel of the room by helping to bring the outside in.*

Blankets and throws *A room always benefits from the introduction of texture, meaning there should always be something handmade, something natural and something elemental. Use a throw to soften up a chair made from wood or metal (or temporarily conceal areas in need of repair). This adds both texture and an extra level of comfort.*

A neutral sofa *Neutral colours do not automatically have to look cold or sterile, as this sofa demonstrates. This sofa, made with a neutral-coloured fabric, adds natural texture and comfort to the space.*

Fireplace *Floor-to-ceiling fireplaces built from natural stone are often a key feature of mid-century modern living rooms.*

Earthenware and ceramics *Earthenware and other ceramics, particularly those produced in Scandinavian countries, are another wonderful way of adding natural elements to any room. Hand-thrown works, such as those shown here, are an elegant way of bringing this beautiful element to your room. Pieces by Swedish master ceramist Carl-Harry Stålhane and fellow Swede Stig Lindberg are great starting points for those looking to add handmade texture and colour to their living room.*

Coffee table *Coffee tables are obviously great for putting things on or using as a focal point for a living room, but they also provide a great opportunity for introducing a little extra storage space. This three-drawer unit does that while making the overall appearance of the table more interesting.*

Signature colours

In the mid-century home of the 1950s and 1960s, entertaining became a popular pastime. From this point, the living room was no longer just a family gathering space but also a social space, and you should keep this dual function in mind when choosing the colour scheme for your own mid-century modern living room.

The use of colour in this living room is characteristic of the mid-century modern style. The overall scheme has been kept relatively simple, with a muted palette of creams and beiges. Natural wood furnishings add warmth and texture. This room is a great example of a key design principle: once the scene is set with a neutral palette, you have the scope to introduce an array of colours using accessories. In this case, the oranges, blues, golds and greens of the light features, glassware and wall art give this space character. The unusual coffee table adds a rustic look to the otherwise clean lines of the room and its furnishings. This quirky living room is a great example of how the mid-century modern style can be reworked slightly with the addition of just a couple of objects to create something which adheres to the aesthetics of the style while at the same time reflecting one's personal tastes.

Bertoia bench

Italian–American artist and designer Harry Bertoia, who is also well known for his stunning metal sculptures, designed a handful of furniture items for Knoll, all of which are still in production. In 1952, at the age of 37, Bertoia designed his iconic Diamond Chair for Knoll. This elegant chair was unique in that it introduced industrial wire mesh as a material in furniture manufacturing, and has become the signature piece by which Bertoia is best known. However, this bench, which was designed in the same year as the Diamond Chair, and was the first piece designed by Bertoia for Knoll, is arguably his most versatile work.

Made from enamelled steel with teak slats, this simple but attractive piece of furniture was designed to be used inside the house or as sturdy patio furniture. The steel legs and supporting frame foreshadow the construction methods employed by Bertoia in his later work for Knoll and, despite its intended use as a seat, it is also used as a coffee table in many mid-century modern living rooms.

Designer
Harry Bertoia

Manufacturer
Knoll

Year
1952

Place
USA

Materials
Solid wood, welded steel with polished chrome finish, plastic

Dimensions
Height: 41 cm
Width: 168 cm
Depth: 46 cm

175 E Contour low back lounge chair

Vladimir Kagan's sculpted Contour series of furniture was first produced in 1953 by Kagan–Dreyfuss, a New York-based company founded in 1950 by Hugo Dreyfuss and Vladimir Kagan. This chair from the series remains one of the most sensual pieces of modern furniture ever created. With fluid, curvilinear styling, the Contour lounge chair seems to eschew modern design manifestos by existing simply to look good. The show-stopping Contour range included a recliner, a lounge chair, a chaise, a rocker and even a foot stool.

This chair garnered many celebrity fans including Gary Cooper, Marilyn Monroe and Lily Pons; Kagan wanted the person sitting in the chair to look as good as the chair itself. Wrapped in fluid upholstery and beautifully crafted from walnut, the chair made the sitter part of a functional sculpture. This chair is a relatively late addition to the 'icon' world, but alongside the resurgent interest in mid-century modern design, the Contour range has gained a new adoring audience.

Designer
Vladimir Kagan

Manufacturer
Kagan–Dreyfuss

Year
1953

Place
USA

Materials
American walnut, leather

Dimensions
Width: 76 cm
Depth: 89 cm
Height: 86 cm
Seat height: 39 cm

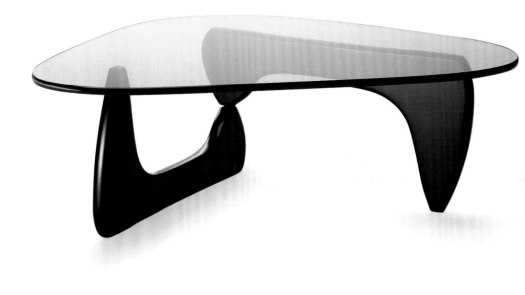

IN-50 coffee table

For some people, there is a blurred line between ubiquitous and iconic, and perhaps it can be argued that modern design classics that appear to be everywhere have lost some of their shine. Critics might point to Isamu Noguchi's IN-50 coffee table as a case in point. Yes, it is a very popular piece, far more so in recent years, but its popularity is what makes this table an icon of design. Expertly conceived and beautifully executed, for many it is the only coffee table they will ever want. Its timelessness is not diminished by its popularity.

Designed by Japanese–American sculptor Isamu Noguchi in 1944, and first produced by Herman Miller, the IN-50 strikes an ethereal balance between art and design, sculpture and practicality. The free-form glass top keeps the sculpted wooden base in view so, as well as being a functional piece of furniture, the table looks like a work of art.

Few have understood organic form better than Noguchi and there was no medium with which he was not comfortable. For Noguchi, who once said 'Everything is sculpture,' there was no transition between design and sculpture. Few objects are more closely associated with their designer; in fact the manufacturer, Herman Miller, no longer calls it the IN-50 but refers to it simply as the Noguchi Table.

Designer
Isamu Noguchi

Manufacturer
Herman Miller

Year
1944

Place
USA

Materials
Birch, glass, aluminium

Dimensions
Width: 128.5 cm
Depth: 92.5 cm
Height: 40 cm

Royal System® shelving unit

The adjustable shelving unit is synonymous with mid-century modern design. Functional and attractive, modular wall units were one of the first pieces of mid-century modern design to become re-popularized following the renewed interest in post-war modernism. They come in many styles, from simple Italian designs to more complex versions with hundreds of attachable options. They are a practical way to display objects, hold books and provide storage. Some models even include bar cupboards and record or magazine holders. Most are mounted on the wall and sold in panels. One can buy a single panel or several, depending on individual requirements. Each attachable modular piece can fit onto any panel of the unit.

One of the most popular of these wall unit systems was the Royal System®, designed by Poul Cadovius of Denmark. The first design for the Royal System® was presented in 1948. These original versions offered a simple solution to design and storage needs. After winning medals, the design of the Royal System® began to evolve, with more and more options made available. While most were open-backed, some were attached to the wall with full-sized sheets of wood veneer that created a luxurious statement. Available in teak, rosewood or walnut, the Royal System® is undoubtedly one of the most successful mid-century modern designs ever created, and the demand for this practical shelving system has never been greater.

Designer
Poul Cadovius

Manufacturer
DK3

Year
1948

Place
Denmark

Materials
Oak, black stained oak, walnut or BauBuche with raw brass or stainless-steel hangers

Dimensions
Various

Praying Mantis floor lamp

In contemporary design circles, floor lamps have become less popular than in past decades. The comfortable reading area, well lit with an attractive floor lamp, seems to be less in fashion. However, every good mid-century modern living room needs a floor lamp. A period floor lamp can be a strong and effective statement piece, or it can be a simple and utilitarian object, happy to just do its job and not draw attention to itself. Whatever your taste and needs, there is a mid-century modern floor lamp for every style.

One of the most unique and instantly recognizable floor lamps was this one, created by French designer Jean Rispal and produced by his own company in France in the 1950s. Taking his inspiration from childhood memories and the works of artists and poets, Rispal was an unusual designer with a strong personal vision of what design could be. Turning his back on the academic 'isms' of the day, he produced striking lamp designs that seem to be alive. The Praying Mantis floor lamp is no exception. A beautifully rendered piece, this lamp is supported by a sculptural mahogany frame and was available with several different shades, each designed for different uses. A bold and commanding statement, this lamp demonstrates the vast variety of styles and approaches used by the designers of the mid-century modern period.

Designer
Jean Rispal

Manufacturer
Rispal

Year
1950s

Place
France

Materials
Walnut, brass, plastic

Dimensions
Height: 160 cm

2213 sofa

Aficionados would likely claim that the Børge Mogensen sofa is not a superstar piece sought after by collectors, but it perfectly embodies the design aesthetic of early 1960s mid-century modernism. Like many of his contemporaries, Danish-born Mogensen started out as a cabinetmaker before training as a furniture designer and ultimately an architect. His journey through the trades is clearly reflected in the build quality of his pieces, and his perfectly proportioned sofas, alongside his notable chair and table designs, are capable of providing the centrepiece of any mid-century modern living room.

Børge Mogensen sofas have been manufactured by Danish firm Fredericia Stolefabrik since their introduction in 1962 and are still in production today. Similarly styled sofas made by firms such as Stouby and Mogens Hansen offer high-quality alternatives at a slightly lower price point for the budget conscious, but the original Børge Mogensen Select Collection cannot be beaten in terms of the quality of the materials used in their manufacture. Solid teak, walnut or oak, is combined with high-grade leather, and backed by a layer of heavy-duty linen. The leather cushions are stuffed with goose down.

Designer
Børge Mogensen

Manufacturer
Fredericia Stolefabrik

Year
1962

Place
Denmark

Materials
Hardwoods (teak, oak or walnut), linen, leather

Dimensions
Height: 80 cm
Length: 221 cm
Depth: 81 cm

COOKING

The kitchen

In the mid-century modern home, the kitchen is undoubtedly one of the most used rooms in the house. Subsequently, it has to be well built and carefully designed to stand the rigours of daily life. Today, more people will eat their meals in the kitchen than the dining room. In the mid 20th century this was an emerging trend that the designers and architects of the time were preparing for. They carefully considered natural and task lighting to create an inviting and warm space, quality work surfaces and storage to keep them free from clutter, and the ergonomics of the work space, calculating 'work paths' that would make the kitchen experience more efficient. Manufacturers were also producing countless 'labour-saving' devices and appliances that would speed up cooking and cleaning, freeing up valuable time. The kitchen was now an integral part of family life. Over the course of twenty years, the kitchen in the mid-century modern home went from being basic and utilitarian to a well-designed and well-engineered work and living space. Many of the lessons learned by mid-century modern designers can be applied today in the contemporary kitchen.

▲ *It is possible to create entirely authentic period kitchen interiors, but give a thought to how you might incorporate newer, energy-efficient appliances.*

▶ *A mid-century modern-style kitchen in an apartment in Glasgow's West End. It includes ample storage and surfaces that are easy to wipe clean. The carefully presented accessories complete the mid-century modern look.*

Efficient and well-functioning

In a mid-century modern kitchen, the idea of pots and pans hanging from an overhead rack and counter surfaces cluttered with appliances was something designers would not abide. With this in mind, they accepted the challenge of making an efficient and well-functioning kitchen. Some designers even created built-in appliances, such as fold-out toasters and tuck-away breadboxes, in an attempt to keep surfaces clear. If the aim was to eliminate clutter, then there was a need for plenty of storage space. The simple aesthetic of the

mid-century modern period meant the long banks
of minimally designed storage cupboards would
work seamlessly in the kitchen space. The
approach remains true today. Whether you choose
a natural material or one of many newer materials,
always keep the cupboard material simple.

Flooring

A kitchen floor should be simple, practical and
durable. If a kitchen has natural elements, such as
wood and stone, a neutral floor is always the best
option. With the newer engineered flooring options
available today there are many options suited to
the mid-century modern style and your own needs.

Accessories

Today, the mid-century modern kitchen is all about the accessories. We no longer use the energy-inefficient stoves and refrigerators of the period, and nor should we. However, it is possible to create the feeling of the era with a few simple additions that will liven up the kitchen and create a mid-century modern vibe. Items like Jens Quistgaard's pepper mills and ice buckets, and Kobenstyle cookware – which were tremendously popular during the period – are an almost essential part of the mid-century modern kitchen. Colourful Cathrineholm enamelware by Grete Prytz Kittelsen can also make a bold statement and recreate the feeling of the era.

In addition to the accessories, the 'breakfast bar' was born during the mid-century modern period, and there are numerous bar stools designed during the 1950s and 1960s that can work wonderfully, even those originally designed for cocktail bars.

To top it off, all good mid-century modern kitchens require a wall clock and, unlike the wall clock one might use in the entrance that often is a bit more formal, the kitchen wall clock can be fun and colourful. Adding just a few mid-century modern items can be transformative.

Storage

While it's important for some labour-saving kitchen equipment to remain on display in the mid-century modern kitchen, it's equally important to ensure that clutter is eliminated. Modular units with clean lines and well distributed storage space designed to accommodate the largest pots as well as the smallest items of cutlery are essential. Kitchen islands and benches designed with hidden under-surface storage provide additional opportunities to incorporate smart storage solutions into any modern kitchen layout.

Lighting

With the advent of kitchen 'design' – where the modern layout of a kitchen was planned more carefully around preparing, eating and socializing – lighting became much more integral to the success of any scheme. Task lighting – lighting which is designed to increase illumination where it is most needed in order to accomplish specific tasks – has become a feature of most modern kitchens since the mid-century modern period. Strip-lighting fixed beneath wall-mounted storage was used extensively to directly illuminate work surfaces, eliminating the problem of shadows cast over the working area by centrally positioned ceiling lights. Freely adjustable spot-lighting, mounted to the wall or ceiling, can also help to reduce the need for general lighting across the whole kitchen.

Case study

Designer AB design studios > **Year** 2012 > **Place** California, USA

Much of modern design was defined by architects who had begun to consider the home as more than merely a place to live, eat and sleep, but rather a space to be engineered. With modern architecture now available to the average consumer, many architects now found themselves designing kitchens not just for the staff of the wealthy, but for those who were actually going to use them. As the kitchen was going to be one of the most used rooms in the house, it would also have to withstand the rigours of daily life. The aim was to make the day-to-day lives of people more convenient and a bit easier.

This approach was one of organization and de-cluttering, and it is what helped form the enduring legacy of mid-century modern design. We can see a wonderfully executed example in this kitchen. Here, ample storage and large, uncluttered surfaces provide an elegant and efficient space. The breakfast bar is also a classic example of mid-century modern design, as casual dining became a regular occurrence in the kitchen.

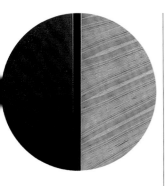

Materials and texture A good design sometimes needs to be an exercise in contrast. To set off the clean, simple lines of this kitchen, a stylish black side-panel has been added to set against the natural wood. The black counter tops also contrast elegantly with the central island and wooden units and cupboards.

Clean, simple cabinetry An adequate amount of cupboard and storage space is essential in any kitchen. Here we see simple but elegant cupboards that are not distracting. Handles are discreet and the outer surfaces are flush with adjacent appliances.

Functional, clutter-free surfaces The clean lines of a typical mid-century modern kitchen can be ruined by unnecessary clutter, and it is a shame to cover a beautiful wood or marble work surface. Carefully designed storage spaces are essential if clutter is to be successfully avoided.

Island unit Perhaps a natural transition from the traditional large farmhouse table where a cook would normally work, the island unit with built-in appliances is a feature popularized during the mid-century modern period, and has endured as an element of many contemporary kitchen designs.

Breakfast bar Hugely popular during the mid-century modern period, this breakfast bar offers a pleasant contrast to the clean angles of the main kitchen area with its rounded ends and chamfered edges.

Task lighting Whether it's stylish pendant lights above a breakfast bar or table, or spotlights sited above work surfaces or walkways, there's little room for error when working with lighting in the kitchen. This room hits all the right notes. The recessed spot lights (very popular during the mid-century modern era) and pendant lights over the breakfast bar are not original mid-century modern features, but work very well as functional objects and do not in any way diminish the mid-century charm of the room.

Signature colours

In the 1950s and 1960s, the kitchen went from utilitarian service area to carefully planned hub of daily life. In response to this demand, the call went out to manufacturers to come up with new, often colourful, materials to suit the needs of modern family living. Counter tops, appliances and cookware went from dreary to dramatic.

With present-day trends making the kitchen not only a space for gathering and entertaining but also one of new technical marvels, it does seem that some of the mid-century exuberance has left our kitchens to be replaced with cool whites, sleek blacks and neutral greys. While it is true these colours were also popular during the mid-century modern period, there was also a penchant for more vitality in the kitchens of fifty or sixty years ago.

The bright yellow walls of this kitchen make a bold statement in a room where mid-century and new technology blend seamlessly. The period furniture sits in front of shiny appliances that are clearly up-to-the-minute, and the extractor above the cooker is cleverly hidden behind a semi-opaque glass screen built with a typically mid-century modern curve.

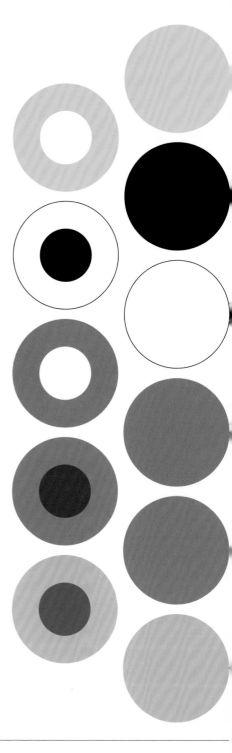

Congo Model 810 ice bucket

Perhaps no other Danish designer was as prolific as Jens Quistgaard. Between his work in furniture, silverware, jewellery, household items and cookware, he left a legacy of over 4,000 designed items. Quistgaard's breakthrough as an industrial designer came in 1953 when he designed the Fjord cutlery set, the first to combine stainless steel with teak handles. In 1954, after several exhibits and awards, Quistgaard was discovered by American businessman Ted Nierenberg, who was scouting Europe for designs he could launch in the United States. After seeing the Fjord cutlery set at the Danish Museum of Art and Design in Copenhagen, Nierenberg had a meeting with Quistgaard, which led to the founding of the company Dansk. The output of Dansk was staggering and eagerly embraced by the public.

Made mostly from teak, but sometimes rosewood, the staved Congo ice bucket is perhaps the most popular of the sculpted items Quistgaard designed for Dansk. In a 1963 newspaper advertisement, the company claimed to have sold a very precise 26,412 of them, an average of about 3,300 per year. Since its release in 1955, it has become an icon of Danish modern design. These buckets provide owners with an affordable way of bringing an attractive, organic element to their kitchen.

Designer
Jens Quistgaard

Manufacturer
Dansk Designs

Year
1955

Place
Denmark

Materials
Teak

Dimensions
Height: 39 cm
Width: 19 cm
Depth: 19 cm

Krenit bowl

A Krenit bowl is often featured on a table top in a typical mid-century modern-styled interior shot. This series was designed by Herbert Krenchel, whose research focused primarily on materials and fibre reinforcement while studying for his Masters in engineering at the Technical University of Denmark. Using a relatively uniform design approach, the bowls are made from steel with a glazed, enamelled lining. The brightly coloured linings of the bowls, a key feature of all Krenit products, set off the uniformly darker exteriors beautifully, and provide owners with numerous options for expanding their collections.

The iconic bowls were first manufactured by Torben Ørskov of Denmark in 1953 and met with immediate success, going on to win the gold medal at the 1954 Milan Triennale. Sold originally as kitchenware, the Krenit bowl has found its way onto shelves and surfaces in every room of the house and is still available today, having recently been relaunched by Normann Copenhagen. To celebrate the iconic status of the Krenit bowl, an accompanying range of variously sized steel and silicone jugs, which Krenchel designed in 1966, has also added to the series.

Designer
Herbert Krenchel

Manufacturer
Originally Torben Ørskov, today produced by Normann Copenhagen

Year
1953

Place
Denmark

Materials
Steel, melamine

Dimensions
Various

Model 61 bar stool

Erik Buch was a Danish designer working in the mid-century modern period, but he sometimes flies below the radar of history, frequently overshadowed by the big-name Scandinavian designers. With more than thirty commercially successful designs throughout his career, there is none better known than his Model 61 bar stool. It was designed in 1961 and first manufactured by Odense Maskinsnedkeri. These beautifully sculpted stools, with their elegantly formed, leather-upholstered seats, were originally made from teak and rosewood. Buch's Model 61 was an instant success and became a common sight in homes throughout the world. The stool is still manufactured today under licence and is a beautiful addition to any kitchen.

Designer
Erik Buch

Manufacturer
Odense Maskinsnedkeri

Year
1961

Place
Denmark

Materials
Walnut or oak, leather

Dimensions
Height: 77 cm
Width: 38 cm
Depth: 45 cm

bulthaup b2 kitchen

Acquiring a mid-century modern property complete with an authentic built-in kitchen that doesn't need attention is a big ask, so a newly manufactured option is a likely consideration for new homeowners. German kitchen manufacturer bulthaup, founded in 1949 by Martin Bulthaup, has for many years manufactured kitchen furniture that combines perfectly with the functional and ergonomic aesthetic of mid-century modernism.

Since launching the Style 75 product range in 1969, the company has stuck to a rigid philosophy of creating high-quality, highly functional, design-led products with a contemporary mid-century modern look. Their system 25 range set a benchmark for modular kitchen design which still stands today. The contemporary slant comes from the use of materials such as durable through-dyed laminates that can be joined to create the impression that worktops are made from a single block of material.

The company's b system product ranges, designed by EOOS, form the backbone of their current offering, with the b2 system arguably offering the option that sails closest to mid-century modern philosophy. The system is inspired by the idea that 'tools and materials must always be kept tidy and close at hand', and comprises a central workbench, a kitchen-tool cabinet and a second cabinet that houses appliances that are neatly hidden when not in use.

Designer
EOOS

Manufacturer
bulthaup

Year
2000s

Place
Germany

Materials
Oak or walnut, stainless steel, stone

Dimensions
Various

DINING

The dining room

When approaching the design of a room, function always comes first. A dining room is clearly going to need a table, chairs, a sideboard and appropriate mood and task lighting. Everything else is left to the imagination of the owner.

The mid-century modern dining room can on occasion seem to be the most utilitarian room of a house. This is explained largely by those functional requirements, but can also be put down to the fact that it is seen as a more formal dining option when compared to everyday meals consumed by families in the kitchen, or perhaps even on trays in front of the TV.

Lighting

Dining-room lighting must be well considered. Serving as the venue for both intimate and social gatherings, a dining room must have multifunctional lighting. The preferred choice of lighting is a low-hanging pendant lamp, but not so low that it obstructs the view of the guests sitting at the table. It was by creating lighting for the dining room that many designers of this period hit their stride, producing well-designed and elegant lamps, many of which were like jewellery for the ceiling. This is how dining-room lighting should be considered; like a piece of jewellery that will perfectly complement your outfit. One must take scale into account when choosing dining room lighting. The light must fit the space and not be too big or small. Trust your eye when choosing. As in all things, it is all about balance.

Sideboards

A sideboard is as mid-century modern as it gets, and is a key requirement in any dining room. Offering storage and a working surface, sideboards are functional as well as decorative. The breadth of

▲ Low-hanging pendant lighting must be set at a height that doesn't obstruct the view of other diners around the table.

▶ Sideboards are a necessary component of a mid-century modern dining room.

◄ *A matched set of table and chairs will provide a visually cohesive look for any dining space, although matching is not necessarily essential.*

► *A well-chosen piece of wall art can make a bold statement in a dining room.*

styles and sizes made during the era, particularly in the Scandinavian countries, is staggering. The upside of this tremendous output is that it's relatively easy to find a period sideboard for a reasonable price. A good sideboard can be used to store many items ordinarily stored in the kitchen, such as flatware, tableware, glassware and linens. A well-chosen piece can perfectly set the tone of the dining room. It can also be a great visual base from which to choose your wall art, and a helpful surface for secondary task lighting.

Dining table and chairs

A mid-century modern dining table and chairs are possibly the most omnipresent items of furniture one might come across in any design-conscious home. The reasons for this are, firstly, that practically every notable designer from the period designed at least one dining chair, with individuals such as Hans J. Wegner producing many different designs throughout their careers. This means there are lots of original objects to source, and dining chairs tend to fall into the slightly more affordable spectrum, as opposed to larger items such as sideboards or sofas.

Secondly, while it's desirable to locate and purchase a matching set of table and chairs, it is relatively easy to pair up a table with an unmatched set of dining chairs by another designer which will still work perfectly well together. Recent years have also seen a number of revivals, with contemporary manufacturers building high-quality tables and chairs under licence exactly as they were originally made. Authentic pieces manufactured during the mid-century period carry a patina of age, which is always a desirable factor, but there is a lot to be said for newly revived pieces that have been built to the same exacting standards as the originals.

Artwork

Wall art and other works, such as sculptural pieces of ceramic and wood, are an easy and fulfilling way of imprinting your own personal style onto a space. It is relatively simple to go out and buy matching mid-century modern furniture and set up a working dining room, but this can leave the room feeling a little dull. You should never be timid about experimenting with art and decorative objects. Used sparingly, carefully selected objects such as glasswork and ceramics provide great accents in the dining room.

While it is always preferable to use original artwork when creating a unique space, this is usually costly. One way to acquire original art is to approach local art colleges. Quite often at the end of the school year there are student exhibitions, with many pieces for sale. This is a great opportunity to find good, original pieces of art and it also helps out budding artists.

Case study

Owner Lene Toni Kjeld > **Year(s)** 2010 > **Place** Kolding, Denmark

An adventurous exercise in eclecticism, this dining room pulls no punches. Daring artworks are combined with the simplicity of classic Danish modern design, creating a colourful and intriguing tableau. Some might suggest that this space is a bit over the top. In fact, it could be argued that this room's style is counter to the mid-century modern credo of simplicity. If we were to strip away the artwork in this room, what may seem at first a rather busy space is, in fact, a room consisting of simple pieces of furniture that do not compete with each other. However, removing the artwork would also leave the room lacking in character. If we consider this space carefully, it is easy to see that there is a larger design agenda at play.

The curvilinear style of these elegant chairs contrasts with the bold accessories on display. What may seem like an eclectic mix of pieces works together here because each in its own way is well-designed and functional.

The pendant lights complement the neutral colour of the walls. This might have been a dull choice, but the addition of the bright wall art transforms this by reflecting a warm glow over the dining area. This is a very clever example of art as functional object. Note the addition of a classic Alvar Aalto birch-veneer stackable stool next to the sideboard, for any unexpected dinner guests.

Pendant light *Pendant lighting above the table is a signature feature of the mid-century modern dining room. These particular lights are rather quirky but they work in the overall scheme of the room, which mixes traditional mid-century style with the owner's personal tastes.*

Kubus candleholder *The Kubus candleholder was designed by Mogens Lassen in 1962 and is a design classic. The lacquered metal holder is available in black, white, and brass, copper or nickel plate. The design concentrates the soft light of (in this example) six candles into a smaller area.*

Cylinda Line coffee pot *Arne Jacobsen's 1967 Cylinda Line coffee pots are still produced today by Danish firm Stelton. This example, the AJ press coffee maker, was the first design to be manufactured and is the best known of the range. It's an elegant, sculptural object that demands to be displayed as well as used.*

Form-fitting seating *Advancements in plastic moulding techniques led designers from the mid-century modern period to experiment extensively with new materials. Even today, curved, form-fitting dining chairs can create a fresh look for any dining room where mid-century is the point of reference.*

Alvar Aalto stool *Alvar Aalto's simple yet functional three-legged, stackable stool was designed between 1932 and 1933 but remains a stalwart of many modern interiors. Today it is produced by Finnish company Artek.*

Flooring *Wooden flooring, whether boarded or laid as a laminate, is an essential component of any mid-century modern dining space. Stone or polished concrete floors can work just as well, but the warmth of a wooden floor adds to the social feel of a dining space.*

Signature colours

Whether it's a lively family dinner, an intimate meal, or even serving as a makeshift office, the dining room can be called on to perform multiple functions. How do you choose a colour palette that works for this versatile space? Colour affects mood and the mood of a successful dining space is one of conviviality, warmth and intimacy, which is why warm and earthy tones tend to work best.

Underscoring this room is a pale marbled floor which works well with the white dining furniture and doesn't compete with the otherwise warm tones in the room. When using honey tones or medium-warm browns as a base there are a considerable number of complementary colours to choose from. The wonderful built-in display cabinet seen here showcases carefully chosen objects, which are both decorative (for example, the vase) and practical (wine glasses and drinks), in cool and relaxing tones. The cabinet also creates a frame for the table and chairs.

This room works on many levels. It is contemporary while still maintaining a typical mid-century modern character, and mixes styles to create an individual impression. The use of a unified colour palette enhances and links these design traits.

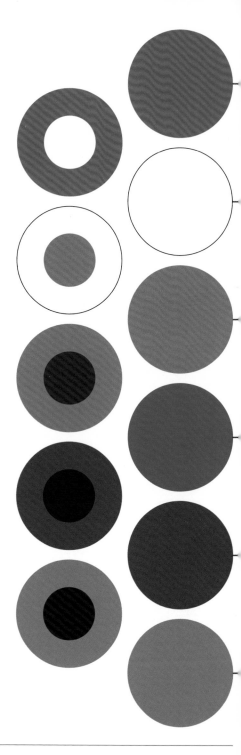

MFL-3 standing lamp

Almost insect-like in appearance, the Serge Mouille standing lamp was this designer's reaction to the plethora of Italian lamps that seemed ubiquitous throughout the world in the 1950s. Mouille, who believed in minimalism, felt the lamp designs of his Italian contemporaries were far too fussy and complicated. Commissioned by French gallerist Steph Simon, and only manufactured for two years, these Mouille lamps were available at the time in several variations and models, which are rare and in high demand.

Today, Mouille lamps are far from affordable, with most models selling at auction for tens of thousands of pounds. If you lack the budget for such an expenditure there are other options. Companies such as Lightolier of the United States produced hundreds of dining room light fixtures, some similar in style to the Mouille and much more affordable. There are inexpensive copies of many of the Mouille lamps, but it is always preferable to buy an original period fixture with superior build quality.

The three-armed version is the most versatile lamp of the Mouille collection. Each arm rotates so the shades can be oriented independently to suit the space. Revival editions are available in black or white, with a line-mounted floor switch, from Guéridon of the United States.

Designer
Serge Mouille

Manufacturer
Serge Mouille Editions

Year
1952

Place
France

Materials
Aluminium, steel

Dimensions
Height: 210 cm
Width: 133.5 cm
Depth: 145 cm

Carl-Harry Stålhane ceramics

The Swedes have a tremendous history of producing fine ceramic ware (as they do with glass) and one of their best makers was Carl-Harry Stålhane. Born in 1920 in Mariestad, Sweden, Stålhane began working at the Rörstrand ceramic works in 1939, when he was nineteen years old, taking a brief break to study in Paris at the Académie Colarossi from 1947 to 1948. By the time he was thirty, Stålhane was already a master ceramist. His best works were produced by Rörstrand, with whom he maintained a fifty-year working relationship.

In the late 1940s, Stålhane was promoted to art director and chief designer of Rörstrand, taking over from his teacher and mentor Gunnar Nylund. In the early 1960s his attention was drawn towards larger, more rugged forms with thick and quickly applied glazes. For the next several years he would experiment with different clays found in the rich soils surrounding Rörstrand, with chemistry, colour and application techniques. Stålhane was constantly searching for new challenges. This may be why in 1973, after forty years, he left his position at Rörstrand and opened his own studio, Designhuset, with the assistance of master thrower and friend Kent Ericsson. Continuing his artistic development, Stålhane's later works reflected his interest in Chinese and Japanese pottery, which had always fascinated him. Carl-Harry Stålhane died in 1990, leaving behind a prolific body of work much sought after today by collectors.

Designer
Carl-Harry Stålhane

Manufacturer
Rörstrand

Year
1950s and 1960s

Place
Sweden

Materials
Ceramic

Dimensions
Various

Sputnik chandelier

This lamp is a rare example of an object that is so clearly reminiscent of its era that it is almost a cliché. This is not necessarily a bad thing. The assortment of 'Sputnik' lamps that were available in the late 1950s and 1960s was astounding. Several manufacturers produced their own version of the lamp, which was said to have been inspired by the first satellite in space, the USSR's *Sputnik 1*, launched in October 1957. Nevertheless, the origins of this style of lamp date to quite some time before the Soviet satellite was launched. Prior to the Second World War, Italian designers were experimenting with similar lighting forms. For example, Gino Sarfatti's Model 2003 Fuoco d'Artificio ('Fireworks') ceiling light was designed in 1939, almost twenty years before the American lamps were introduced. However, due to the outbreak of the Second World War, which halted a great deal of new consumer goods production in Italy, particularly those involving metalwork, Sarfatti's 'Fireworks' lamp would not enter the market until it was produced by Arteluce in the early 1950s. Today, the Sarfatti-designed lamp would be very expensive, but a good period Sputnik lamp can be found for a fair price.

Designer
Unknown

Manufacturer
Lightolier

Year
1960s

Place
USA

Materials
Chrome

Dimensions
Height: 91 cm
Width: 61 cm
Depth: 61 cm

Model 116 sideboard

Groundbreaking architect and designer Florence Knoll, who studied under Ludwig Mies van der Rohe and Eliel Saarinen, took full control of Knoll Inc. after her husband Hans Knoll died in a car accident in 1955. Knoll went on to create some of the best design icons of the 20th century. After taking over at the helm of Knoll, with her eye set on international growth for the company, Florence embarked on an ambitious plan to introduce new designs. To say that she succeeded would be an understatement. Today, Knoll International is one of the world's largest producers of modern furniture, with many design icons to its name, including pieces designed by Eero Saarinen, Harry Bertoia, and Mies van der Rohe.

It is, however, Florence Knoll's own designs that perhaps best express her desire for simple, functional and attractive furniture. Following the lesson of her mentor Mies van der Rohe, Knoll's pieces are the epitome of a minimalist design philosophy. Her sideboards are the best example of this. Perfectly proportioned, the basic form is a simple rectangle, normally supported by inset metal legs. Texture and warmth are brought to the piece by Knoll's careful choice of woods, sometimes accompanied by a seagrass-covered door. An interesting signature of a Knoll sideboard is a folded piece of leather that functions as the cabinet's handle. The overall impact is one of understated beauty, rendered perfectly in the simplest lines.

Designer
Florence Knoll

Manufacturer
Knoll International

Year
1952

Place
USA

Materials
Teak, steel, seagrass, leather

Dimensions
Height: 77.5 cm
Width: 180 cm

Eye dining chair

There are many great Danish designers, such as Wegner, Volther, Juhl, Kofod-Larsen, and Kjærholm, whose works are recognizable to most fans of modernism and have gone on to define Scandinavian modern. However, there is one designer whose extensive body of work is perhaps better known than he is. Ejvind A. Johansson's designs, which many consider ahead of their time, epitomize the simple but true form of Nordic classicism. Despite this, he is perhaps the least famous great designer of the period. While he may be lacking the cachet of the 'bigger name' designers, Johansson's pieces are much more affordable, but certainly no less beautiful.

Born in 1923, Ejvind Johansson trained in the traditional methods of cabinetmaking and joinery, and then studied at the Royal Danish Academy of Fine Arts, where he graduated in 1949. In 1956 he became the head of design at Fredericia Stolefabrik, and it was here he would create the Eye, one of his most beautiful works.

Commonly known as the Eye because of its distinctively sculpted backrest, the chair went relatively unnoticed until recently, when examples began showing up at auction. The bold design of the chair, manufactured by Gern in 1961, is quite unique. It makes a bold statement for a mid-century modern-style dining room.

Designer
Ejvind A. Johansson

Manufacturer
Gern

Year
1961

Place
Denmark

Materials
Teak, leather

Dimensions
Height: 77 cm
Width: 50 cm
Depth: 48 cm

Pyramid table and Result chair

The Pyramid table and Result chair provide an interesting example of how mid-century modern furniture can seamlessly integrate into more than one room in your home or workplace. Friso Kramer and Wim Rietveld, the son of the famous Dutch designer and architect Gerrit Rietveld, were working for office furniture specialists Ahrend in the late 1950s when they designed the Pyramid table and its complementary Result chair. Both pieces were designed to be light but strong (and stackable) and were produced primarily for use in schools throughout the Netherlands during the 1960s and 1970s. It wasn't long before people realized that the practical sheet-steel and oak furniture could also be used for stylish and comfortable dining. The table and chair combination became a domestic hit, particularly in the Netherlands, where the Dutch retained a nostalgic attachment to the furniture of their school days.

If you can't find an original example, both the Pyramid table and Result chair have recently been relaunched in a joint venture by Danish manufacturer and retailer HAY and Ahrend. As a small concession to comfort, HAY have added 15 mm to the height of the table in recognition of its popularity as a piece of dining furniture.

Designer
Friso Kramer and Wim Rietveld

Manufacturer
HAY and Ahrend

Year
1958–1959

Place
Netherlands

Materials
Sheet steel, oak

Dimensions
(table)
Various

(chair)
Height: 81 cm
Width: 45.5 cm
Depth: 48 cm

CLEANSING

The bathroom

A peculiar quirk of the homes designed and built in the mid-century modern period is that, when it came to the modern design ideology applied so thoroughly to the rest of the home, the bathroom often went overlooked. Consequently, it is not uncommon when looking at photos from the era to be struck by how dated this room appears. It was even a common practice among many of the design and architectural magazines of the period to not include photos of the bathroom at all in their articles.

In the 1950s and 1960s, the basic design of the bathroom relied on the same stock toilets, bathtubs and sinks as found in previous decades, but with newer, more fashionable colours, such as pink, mint green and aqua tones. Modern design for the bathroom in the average mid-century modern home seems to have been overlooked. Architects Richard Neutra and John Lautner were among the exceptions, working with a 'whole living space' philosophy, and did put effort into making the bathroom part of a unified design.

Natural light

Natural light, as well as being environmentally considerate, will always be more pleasant than any other lighting source. A large, clear window in a bathroom might reduce the sense of privacy, so many resort to using textured and frosted glass. However, if the view from the bathroom window happens to be a lush private garden, it seems a shame to block this out. The architects and designers of the mid-century modern period embraced natural lighting. Many homes from this period feature large, floor-to-ceiling windows, which often overlook small inner courtyards filled with greenery.

▲ *Wall-mounted units can make a small bathroom feel a lot more spacious.*

▶ *If you have the space, a vanity unit with a flip-up mirror is a great addition to any mid-century modern bathroom.*

▲ *Contemporary bathroom hardware will create a more luxurious bathing experience. When combined with mid-century modern pieces it will not diminish the overall style of your bathroom.*

Impervious surfaces

Following the Second World War, many manufacturers began experimenting with newer engineered materials to create composites with mica and natural stone. The American company Formica was the leader in these new materials, and offered hundreds of colours and patterns. Their thin, easy-to-apply product was seen on the surfaces of kitchens and bathrooms worldwide. It was also used the world over for various consumer goods. As a durable and affordable product, many of the original Formica patterns have become icons of this period. However, as we will see in our case study bathroom (on the following pages), high-quality, natural materials are always the best choice for bathroom surfaces

Cabinetry/mirrors

According to mid-century modern taste, when it comes to bathroom mirrors, bigger is better. While a full-size wall mirror may not be possible for everyone, there are some great options when it comes to creating a welcoming bathroom space that reflects the style of the mid-century modern period. Scandinavian countries produced a staggering array of cabinets, often with no designer association. Wall-mounted vanities and teak-framed mirrors, made in mid-century Scandinavia, all make excellent accessories for the bathroom. Even the American designers created pieces for the bathroom, such as George Nelson's illuminated, fold-down vanity. Tall hall mirrors from this period, often found in amorphous shapes and framed in teak, walnut or rosewood, make perfect full-length mirrors for the bathroom, and are an excellent way to add natural elements to the room. There is a substantial amount of what some people call 'no name' Scandinavian design that's affordable and can be repurposed for use in the bathroom.

Taps and hardware

It would be nice to have a completely original mid-century modern bathroom. Or would it? As with the kitchen, sixty-year-old appliances and hardware are often not up to today's tasks. If you are someone who appreciates the design, many older taps can be refurbished. The original taps of the mid-century modern period were often chunky, with soft, angular designs, and if this suits your tastes these can be obtained, ready for refurbishment, from any good architectural salvage dealer. However, these will not come with a guarantee, so it is perhaps better to upgrade. There are various styles of new taps that would work very well in a mid-century modern bathroom, and will be more efficient than the taps of fifty or sixty years ago. If authenticity is important to you, many companies today produce reissues, but these are very expensive and often border on kitsch.

Accessories

In any bathroom, you will need space for everyday items. While the mid-century modern credo of an uncluttered space may be easy to apply to a living room or bedroom, the bathroom has its own unique challenges. Fortunately, there are many mid-century modern accessories that, while not originally intended for the bathroom, work wonderfully here. For example, simple ceramic bowls are great for holding smaller objects, while large pieces work well for storing towels. Even a magazine rack could work beautifully as storage in a bathroom. The trick is to keep your choices within the same general colour palette. When choosing your accessories, neutral ceramics and natural woods will always work well, or if there is an existing colour scheme, choose muted and softer variations on these colours. A simple walk through a flea market or good second-hand shop can unearth many great period pieces that will make your bathroom a more complete space.

Case study

Designer Annika Kampmann > **Year(s)** 2009 > **Place** Saltsjö-Boo, Sweden

The American architect Frank Lloyd Wright adhered to the practice of creating cohesiveness for all the rooms of his buildings, including the bathroom, throughout his illustrious career. His bathrooms were largely custom-built, always keeping in mind the overall look of the home. Wright was fond of built-in seating and custom lighting, and his bathrooms were a practical and stylish addition to the home, and not simply an afterthought as with other designers of the time. Wright's bathrooms used natural materials, such as stone and wood, which make his designs timeless and coherent with the rest of the house.

His love of these materials has influenced generations of designers ever since, as evidenced in this contemporary design, which follows Wright's mid-century modern principles for the bathroom. The room also embraces the elegant and instantly recognizable style of Scandinavian modern. Stone of a consistent colour and texture is used extensively throughout, with the occasional wooden accessory added to the mix to create extra texture and introduce colour. Plants help to bring natural colour, and the large non-frosted glass window and door let light flood in.

Wall mirror *A wall mirror in a bathroom may seem important for obvious reasons, but it can also appear to enlarge the space and increase the amount of available natural light.*

Clear window and door *The large window and door have clear glass, bringing in plenty of natural light. This bathroom benefits from a view over a lush private garden, which this arrangement makes the most of. The effect is that of a calm oasis.*

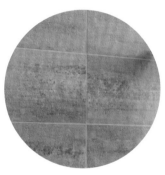

Surfaces *Frank Lloyd Wright had little regard for the artificial, and chose natural materials that were durable and would last the life of the home. Here, granite tiles have been used throughout to this effect.*

Wooden accessories *Together with the beautiful greenery, natural light and neutral palette, the use of wooden accessories, such as the stool, is a complementary choice for this space.*

Signature colours

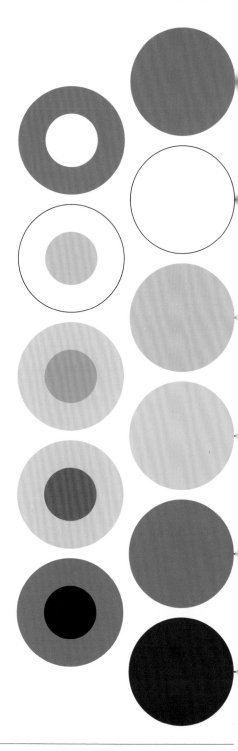

The bathroom is often the room in which people are the most daring in their colour choices. Perhaps bold and bright hues are less intimidating in small spaces, where it's not a big job to change something if it does not work. Whatever the reason, shifting tastes mean that bathrooms are the most frequently renovated spaces in most people's homes, and the evolution of popular colours during the past fifty or so years has never been better displayed than with those chosen for the bathroom. Popular colours have ranged from pink, aqua and mint green in the 1950s to the avocado and browns of the 1970s.

This recently renovated bathroom in a house that dates from the 1960s seems at first glance somewhat limited with its colour palette. A closer inspection, however, reveals that it contains several tones that blend well together to create a welcoming and cohesive space. The tiles chosen for the bath surround contain several shades of green, and some of these tones are picked up and used elsewhere in the room. A light 'icy' green has been used for the sink surround, with a complementary cool grey for the toilet area. A warm, mid-tone brown has been wisely selected for the cabinetry (greens and browns almost always work together), and this has been coupled with a simple, neutral grey floor.

One colour not used here is a soft pink. Pink is not to everyone's taste, of course, but it would work well in this room. It is a surprisingly adaptable colour and, used judiciously, can be a friendly addition to any space.

HV1 mixer tap

Designed in 1968 by Arne Jacobsen, one of Denmark's best-known designers, the HV1 mixer tap originated as part of his commission to design the National Bank building in the centre of Copenhagen. This large building was constructed in several stages, commencing in 1965, and Jacobsen oversaw every aspect of the project up to his death in March 1971.

The idea for the new design of a wall-mounted mixer tap came about after Jacobsen was approached by Verner Overgaard, the owner of VOLA A/S, the company that still manufacturers the HV1 almost fifty years after its creation. Jacobsen's design was used in the new building of the National Bank and has gone on to become one of the most popular mid-century modern tap designs of all time.

With all parts made from solid brass, and some valve housings made from corrosion-free dezincification brass, the taps are designed to last a lifetime and can be purchased in eighteen different finishes or colours. Contemporary models now feature small flow regulators which save water, and electronic versions designed for use in hotels and public spaces can be set to stop the flow automatically as soon as the user's hands move away.

Designer
Arne Jacobsen

Manufacturer
VOLA A/S

Year
1968

Place
Denmark

Materials
Brass

Dimensions
Height: 12 cm
Spout: 11.4 cm

Frame bathroom console

Frame was conceived by Norm Architects for Italian manufacturer EX.T as a flexible system of modular bathroom consoles, and in contemporary terms they conform to a mid-century modern aesthetic, meaning they fit neatly into any bathroom which attempts to follow mid-century design conventions.

The principal steel frame is designed to accommodate a variety of different basin sizes and also incorporates a counter top which can be made from wood, marble or stone. Wooden cabinets or drawer units can be hung in the internal space of the frame, providing a highly customisable unit that is versatile enough to fit in a variety of spaces. Wall-mounted options with clear space beneath are also possible.

While plumbing the unit in clearly fixes its position, the free-standing frame makes positioning in the bathroom space very simple and intuitive.

Designer
Norm Architects

Manufacturer
EX.T

Year
2016

Place
Italy

Materials
Steel, wood, marble, stone

Dimensions
Height: 83 cm
Width: 108.5 cm
Depth: 40 cm

Capelli stool

The Capelli stool is a contemporary creation rather than a mid-century original, but it fits perfectly with the design ethos of mid-century modern style. The fact that it is manufactured by Herman Miller, the company synonymous with mid-century modern furniture, also provides this unique stool with solid mid-century credentials.

Designed in 1999 by Carol Catalano of Boston-based Catalano Design, the Capelli Stool began life as an entry in the triennial International Furniture Design Fair Asahikawa (IFDA). While thinking over new ways to build a better, more comfortable (and visually pleasing) stool, Catalano noticed the shape made by her intertwined fingers and came up with her answer. Cardboard and foam models followed, and a full-scale prototype was completed in two months, taking a silver medal at IFDA.

The stool is manufactured from two identical pieces of shaped plywood, cut with 'fingers' that interlock at the top without the need for any additional fastenings. The resulting structure is extremely strong and stable, comfortable in use, and indeed very pleasing to the eye. The plywood sections are constructed from alternating dark- and light-stained inner plies and finished with a light ash veneer.

Designer
Carol Catalano

Manufacturer
Herman Miller

Year
1999

Place
United States

Materials
Plywood, ash veneer

Dimensions
Height: 43 cm
Width: 40.5 cm
Depth: 33.5 cm

RESTING

The bedroom

Prior to the Second World War, luxury bedrooms with features such as walk-in wardrobes, an en-suite bathroom and private garden were solely the domain of the wealthier classes. In the post-war boom, particularly in the United States, with plentiful resources and the development of suburban housing (which created larger middle-class homes) these luxury amenities became affordable to the working public. Many of these bedrooms featured dressing rooms and large closets with built-in cabinetry and storage. The bedrooms of the modern suburban home were larger, with extra floor space for additional furniture, such as slipper lounge chairs and tables. New technologies in glass manufacturing made it economically feasible to produce large sheets of glass that would become the floor-to-ceiling windows of the period. These windows flooded the bedroom with natural light. The overall result of a well-designed mid-century modern bedroom was a private, restful oasis away from the chores and duties of the rest of the home.

Your calming environment

If there is one room where simplicity and neutral colours have the utmost importance, it would be the bedroom – an intimate space where one should strive for a calm and clutter-free environment, wrapped in a soothing palette. By choosing your lines carefully, understanding complimentary hues and mixing in accessories and smaller items from other periods, you will bring your bedroom to life. It is your bedroom, after all, and it needs to be a space where the rest of the world is put on hold. With help from the timeless elegance of mid-century modern design, it can also be an intimate

▲ *A side table like this Tulip model by Eero Saarinen is a must for the mid-century modern bedroom.*

▶ *Bedside lighting can be directional or ambient, and shades can add splashes of colour to an otherwise calm décor.*

and personal space that will endure for years. Regardless of what items you place in the bedroom, the end result should be calming.

Natural materials

The use of natural materials is paramount in a bedroom. Warm woods like teak, walnut and rosewood are excellent choices and work very well with a broad range of colours and material textures. When working with wood, a general rule is to stick one type for larger furniture pieces and areas. However, this is not a rule carved in stone. Often these days designers will bring a dining-room sideboard into the bedroom, where it can function quite well as added storage. Whatever the approach, natural, warm woods in the bedroom are always going to work.

Lighting

The kitchen needs practical lighting, the living room needs elegant lighting and the bedroom needs both. When it comes to bedroom lamps, the base is generally considered of less importance than the shade. Fabric shades are a wonderful way of adding colour to the room, particularly effective in a room decorated in more neutral palettes. Task lighting for the bedroom should be simple; many mid-century modern homes of the era used recessed spot lights.

▼ *Floor-to-ceiling windows, made economically possible by advances in glass manufacturing during the mid-century period, help to flood bedrooms with natural light.*

Carpeting

The floor of the bedroom should always be warm. Unless you have underfloor heating, a carpet is the best way to achieve this. Deep-pile carpet is a luxurious addition to the bedroom, available in all sizes and colours. One need not buy period, but it is always best to keep the colour low-key and neutral so it does not compete with other items in the room. Deep carpets and rugs became popular in the 1960s and continued to be so in the 1970s. In the early 2000s, they regained some popularity but have since fallen out of trend. However, this is a situation where style trumps trend, and it always will. Deep-pile rugs also function as insulation and will help reduce noise, which is always a welcome bonus in the bedroom.

Additional seating

At the foot of the bed, one could often find a bench with a cushioned or padded top. These low benches provide an ideal spot to place clothes or to simply sit and chat. Popular in the 1950s in the larger bedrooms of the new suburban developments, the bedroom bench is an attractive and functional accessory. Available in countless designs and sizes, most are relatively affordable, can be easily found and, if needed, are simple and inexpensive to reupholster. In fact, finding one that needs some attention is often the most economical approach because one can customize the piece with higher-grade fabric for a more luxurious feel and look. Another popular addition, one that tends to be found more in the American mid-century modern-style home, is a low, armless chair called the slipper chair, which could be sat on for reading or used as a place to leave clothes when getting ready for bed.

Dressing table

It may seem quaint today, but in the mid 20th century small dressing tables, often with fold-up mirrors, would invariably feature in the bedroom. These days, a small desk might serve the same purpose. A desk in the bedroom may seem unconducive to resting, but is a great place to store things and to put down items such as a laptop and phone when on charge.

Soft furnishings

When choosing the drapery, linens and fabric accessories for the bedroom, it is always best to choose neutral colours for larger items, such as curtains and bed coverings, and allow the smaller items, such as pillows and cushions, to provide the necessary pop of colour. Many manufacturers today offer reissues of classic mid-century modern patterns, which will make excellent cushions, pillows and throws to complete the look in your mid-century modern bedroom.

Wall sculpture

Areas of consideration in interior design include colour, light, layout and texture. It is surprising how often texture is overlooked in the design schemes of many rooms. Texture can be achieved through carpets, soft furnishings or accessories, or art. Wall sculpture was very popular during the mid-century modern era, with pieces by Marc Weinstein and Curtis Jeré among the most popular. Commonly used materials included metals such as brass and copper. When choosing wall art, particularly for the bedroom, always keep scale in mind: it should never overwhelm the wall or the room in general.

Case study

Owner Anonymous > **Year(s)** 2013 > **Place** London, UK

A bedroom should be calm and restful for obvious reasons, and designers can sometimes get carried away with the idea that bedrooms should be fairly sterile spaces, using a very limited palette of neutral colours. It is not wrong to do this, of course, but it doesn't have to be the case, as can be seen in this bedroom, which combines those neutral whites and greys with warm yellow hues, dark blue furnishings and a stylish dark-wood sideboard. It is interesting to note that the unit is not a typical piece of bedroom furniture and would look equally at home in the living or dining room.

Accessories have been kept to a minimum to avoid clutter, with just a few books on display. The pendant light sports a fairly lavish shade, but its presence only comes to the fore when the light is switched on. When turned off, the room is returned to its calm state. A simple table lamp provides additional lighting. The classic wooden flooring is softened up by the addition of a rug in a cool, natural colour.

Perhaps the boldest statement in this tranquil room is the wall art hanging above the bed. However, these colours seamlessly blend with those elsewhere in the room. It is possible that the overall look was designed around this painting. This is an interesting and often effective approach.

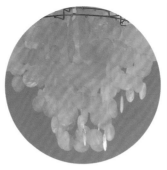

Pendant light *The intricate shade of the pendant light can produce a showy effect when the light is switched on. However, when the light is off the translucent material takes on the warm yellows from the window blind, providing a sense of calm.*

Louvre blinds *In order to filter the amount of light entering the bedroom without creating a full blackout, louvre blinds have been used to allow just enough natural light to enter, thus maintaining the restful atmosphere.*

Minimal accessories *Clutter is of course not desirable with mid-century modern style, especially in the bedroom. This artfully arranged pile of old books is an attractive feature and stops the room feeling too cold and sparse.*

Flooring *The dark staining of the wooden flooring in this bedroom works really well with the overall colour palette of the room, but on its own might look a little austere. The soft woollen rug offsets this and helps ensure the overall look isn't too dark.*

Signature colours

Unlike the dining and living rooms, the bedroom is not a space designed with anyone else in mind besides the individual or couple who will sleep there. Therefore, this is your opportunity to showcase your individuality. What colours do you need to create your personal oasis? Of course, your bedroom should make you feel relaxed, and colour can be applied in a variety of ways to achieve this. Ultimately, however, the decision comes down to personal taste.

Individual taste notwithstanding, the bedroom of the mid-century modern period tended to include neutral colours and natural materials. In this small bedroom, there are three key features: a floor-to-ceiling stone wall; a wood-panelled ceiling with beam; and large glass windows. When a room has wonderful architectural elements, it is usually best to choose paler, neutral wall colours that will not detract from these. However, brighter colours have been introduced successfully here, adding some character to the space. For example, the bright red lamps and the muted blues of the bed cover make the room seem lively despite the otherwise neutral colour scheme. Introducing colour to a room by using accessories in this way is an adaptable approach because such items can easily be changed if desired. The reds and blues may not be to everyone's taste, but they bring character to the space and the tones used still have a warm and cosy feel. Finally, this room is another great example of how the exterior can be made part of the design plan, as the large windows introduce natural greens to the space.

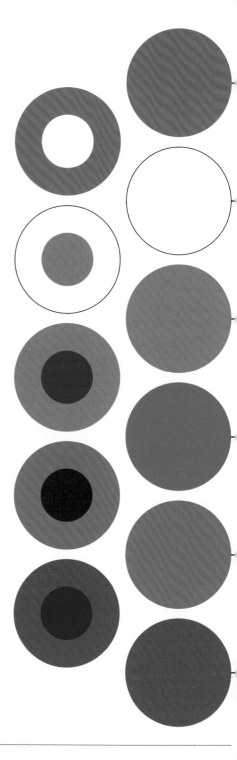

Curtis Jeré Raindrops mirror

Beginning in the late 1950s, sculpted metal wall art became popular in the mid-century modern home, particularly in North America. Often made from copper and brass, quite a few of these pieces were reflective of the abstract and heavily textured sculpture of the time, a good example of which is found in the works of Alberto Giacometti.

One of the biggest producers of sculpted metal wall art was Curtis Jeré. Curtis Jeré was not an individual but rather the compound name of two Americans, Curtis Freiler and Jerry Fels, who formed the company Artisan House in 1963. They produced thousands of pieces over the following decade, but by the 1980s these were considered kitsch and given little regard. The resurgence of mid-century modern has led to a new, appreciative fan base for Curtis Jeré, and today their work is collected by many mid-century modern fans.

Curtis Jeré sculptures are still made today, although the company has changed hands several times since its founding, and the 'authentic' Jeré pieces are now produced in China, rather than the United States. Larger manufacturers and designers have begun making copies of many of the better-known Curtis Jeré designs. Aim to find earlier pieces; if they have enamelling or resin on them, it's a safe bet that they are an original. These are older techniques, which have become expensive and time-consuming, and generally are not used today.

This particular piece is a mirror designed by Curtis Jeré in 1969 for Artisan House.

Designers
Curtis Freiler and Jerry Fels

Manufacturer
Artisan House

Year
1969

Place
USA

Materials
Brass, mirrored glass

Dimensions
Height: 84cm
Width: 84 cm
Depth: 15 cm

Model 9224 table lamp

One of the most effective ways of bringing a quality of warmth to the bedroom is with proper lighting. While many people may be content to simply buy a lamp and not give it much thought beyond whether it lights up, bedside lamps deserve careful attention. A bedside table lamp must provide enough light for basic tasks, such as reading, but it must also be warm and soft. A light turned on in the middle of the night should not be blindingly uncomfortable. The bedside lamp should be just a little bit sensual, and even flirty.

Perhaps no lighting designer was more prolific than Paavo Tynell. Known as 'the man who illuminated Finland', his lighting designs were sophisticated and understated. In 1954 Tynell co-founded lighting company Taito Oy in Finland and worked as its chief designer. During his successful career, he worked with world-renowned designers, including Eliel Saarinen (father of Eero Saarinen), and Alvar Aalto, producing stunning lighting for their architectural projects. Tynell's preferred material was brass. Wonderful patterns of light would be cast into the room via the delicately perforated motifs on the brass shades. As brass would transmit heat easily, he often wrapped the stem of the lamp with tightly rolled cane or leather, creating a beautiful balance of materials. With thousands of designs produced, ranging from the relatively affordable to the very expensive, a Paavo Tynell lamp is a perfect bedroom accessory.

Designer
Paavo Tynell

Manufacturer
Taito Oy

Year
1950s

Place
Finland

Materials
Solid brass, leather

Dimensions
Height: 55 cm
Width: 17 cm
Depth: 24 cm

Joseph-André Motte
vanity cabinet

The idea of a dressing table may seem a little dated today, as most people hurriedly prepare themselves at the bathroom washbasin, but a dressing table in the bedroom is not so out of touch as one might think. Mid-century modern dressing tables would often feature hidden mirrors, revealed by lifting a lid, and would provide an additional working surface. Some of the most beautiful of these period dressing tables were designed by the Scandinavians, but Joseph-André Motte was a French designer who created exquisite versions.

Born in 1925, Joseph-André Motte is considered one of the most influential designers of post-war European modernism. At a time when designers were experimenting with new materials and new methods in design and manufacturing, Motte was not shy about using glass in tables, Formica for surfaces and steel in his furniture pieces, often creating striking contrasts between the natural wood figuring and the glint of chromed steel. Motte designed pieces for the entire home and became not just a furniture designer but an interior designer as well. His flip-up dressing tables are stunningly simple and would work anywhere. If a dressing table is not to your liking in the bedroom, these also make excellent compact desks with useful storage.

Designer
Joseph-André Motte

Manufacturer
Charron

Year
1958

Place
France

Materials
Metal, rosewood

Dimensions
Height: 79 cm
Width: 180 cm
Depth: 51 cm

Jens Risom slipper chair

Following the post-war boom in the United States, housing in the new suburban developments featured larger bedrooms and furniture designers began creating pieces for the bedroom beyond the standard bed and chests of drawers. A popular piece of bedroom furniture in the mid-century modern period became the low, armless slipper chair. These chairs, often sold in pairs, were meant to help create a 'cosy corner' in the bedroom where one could sit and while away some relaxing hours with a good book.

One of the most attractive of the slipper chairs was designed by Jens Risom. Risom, who moved from Denmark to the United States in 1939, had great difficulty finding work until he met Hans Knoll (Florence Knoll's future husband), and in 1941 the two struck up a working partnership, producing several successful designs, most notably Risom's 'strap' lounge chair. By the late 1950s, however, Risom had started his own studio, producing his own designs. His work was a clever mix of the quality craft techniques of his native Denmark with the American aesthetic. His slipper chairs were very popular not just in the bedroom but the living room as well. Risom's name does not carry the sometimes staggeringly high prices of his contemporaries, making his pieces an affordable item to keep an eye out for.

Designer
Jens Risom

Manufacturer
Knoll

Year
1960s

Place
USA

Materials
Maple, wool

Dimensions
Height: 74 cm
Width: 60 cm
Depth: 71 cm

Further resources

Books:

Dominic Bradbury. *Mid-Century Modern Complete*. Thames & Hudson, 2014

Eames Demetrios, *Charles Eames and Ray Eames. Eames: Beautiful Details*. AMMO Books, 2014

Charlotte & Peter Fiell (eds). *Decorative Art 60s*. Taschen, 2013

Charlotte & Peter Fiell (eds). *Decorative Art 50s*. Taschen, 2013

Cara Greenberg. *Mid-Century Modern: Furniture of the 1950s*, Three Rivers Press, 1995

Alan Hess. *Frank Lloyd Wright: The Houses*. Rizzoli, 2005

Wendy Kaplan. *California Design, 1930–1965: "Living in a Modern Way"*. The MIT Press, 2011

Barbara Lamprecht, Julius Shulman and Peter Gössel (Ed.). *Neutra: Complete Works*. Taschen, 2010

Nicholas Olsberg, Jean-Louis Cohen, Frank Escher. *Between Earth and Heaven: The Architecture of John Lautner*. Rizzoli, 2008

Bradley Quinn. *Mid-Century Modern: Interiors, Furniture, Design Details*. Conran, 2006

Julius Shulman, Hunter Drohojowska-Philp, Owen Edwards, Philip J. Ethington, Peter Loughrey. *Julius Shulman: Modernism Rediscovered. (3 vols)*. Taschen, 2007

Websites:

Architonic (for information about design and architecture and designer biographies)
www.architonic.com

Getty Search Gateway (for quality historical images of mid-century modern interiors)
search.getty.edu/gateway/landing

Live Auctioneers (an excellent resource for recent auction results)
new.liveauctioneers.com

Author biography

DC Hillier is an interior designer and collector with a passion for mid-century modern and international modernist design. He has consulted on several publications, and sits on the Collections Committee of the Design Exchange at Canada's Design Museum (www.dx.org).

DC is based in Montreal, Canada, where he runs his website, *MCM Daily* (www.mcmdaily.com).